"As a consultant to thousands of top business leaders around the world, I heartily recommend *Vision-Driven Leadership* to every leader, manager, and aspiring leader or manager who wants to create a growing organization — profit or non-profit. Merrill Oster has broken new ground that could revolutionize the way your organization leads people toward greater effectiveness."

Joe D. Batten, bestselling author
Tough-Minded Leadership

Also by Merrill J. Oster—

Father to Son:
Becoming a Man of Honor

Father to Daughter:
Becoming a Woman of Purpose

Foreword by **KENNETH H. BLANCHARD, Ph.D.**
Co-author of **THE ONE-MINUTE MANAGER**

VISION-DRIVEN
Leadership

MERRILL J. OSTER

Here's Life Publishers

First Printing, February 1991

Published by
HERE'S LIFE PUBLISHERS, INC.
P.O. Box 1576
San Bernardino, CA 92402

Library of Congress Cataloging-in-Publication Data
Oster, Merrill J., 1940-
    Vision-driven leadership : a clear-sighted approach to growing
your organization / Merrill J. Oster.
        p.   cm.
    ISBN 0-89840-284-0
    1. Organizational effectiveness. 2. Business ethics.
3. Management—Moral and ethical aspects. I. Title.
HD58.9088   1990
174'.4—dc20   90-21609
                                              CIP

Cover design by David Marty Design.

For More Information, Write:
L.I.F.E.—P.O. Box A399, Sydney South 2000, Australia
Campus Crusade for Christ of Canada—Box 300, Vancouver, B.C., V6C 2X3, Canada
Campus Crusade for Christ—Pearl Assurance House, 4 Temple Row, Birmingham, B2 5HG, England
Lay Institute for Evangelism—P.O. Box 8786, Auckland 3, New Zealand
Campus Crusade for Christ—P.O. Box 240, Raffles City Post Office, Singapore 9117
Great Commission Movement of Nigeria—P.O. Box 500, Jos, Plateau State, Nigeria, West Africa
Campus Crusade for Christ International—Arrowhead Springs, San Bernardino, CA 92414, U.S.A.

To my business associates
who have dedicated themselves
to continuous improvement.

We are serving, learning and building an
organization which makes a difference in
the eyes of our customers, those wonderful
people around the world who use our
products and services.

My business associates know these
customers are the real "boss."

MISSION OF THIS BOOK

To spell out how value-based, vision-driven organizations build a culture which energizes people and stimulates sustainable growth. To help people unleash reservoirs of energy previously sapped by organizational politics, fear, back-biting, jealousy, hate, empire building and self-centeredism.

CONTENTS

ACKNOWLEDGMENTS

After a year's work in my "spare time," the first manuscript of this book was finally on my desk. I sat dejected. I'm journalist enough to spot second-quality work. This truly wasn't my best effort. I had a vision but I tried to execute it between rush projects, in the wee hours of the morning, on airplane flights—and, yes, even while on "vacation."

I called Steve Bennett, a fellow professional who came alongside and rebuilt the book: writing, rewriting, editing, interviewing me and several of my friends. Six months, dozens of hours of telephone conversations and hundreds of dollars of fax transmissions later, we recreated *Vision-Driven Leadership*. Without Steve, this manuscript would never have seen the eyes of its publisher, Les Stobbe at Here's Life Publishers. Les and his associate, Dan Benson, asked many more questions and gave me several new challenges before my final rewrite. Their input was vital to the finished product.

Thanks, also, to a group of men who allow me to call them friends—the men whose experience and opinions I quote. These are men I've met through the Young Presidents Organization, board memberships and business relationships. In each of their lives is a personal success story. Each of these men has contributed time to this book by making themselves available: Ken Blanchard, Bill Pollard, Bill Schwarz, Bob Denckhoff, Jim Balkcom, Lewis Timberlake, Steve Uhlmann, Bill Benskin, Stew Leonard, Chris Crane, Joe Batten, Bob Buford and Gary Ginter.

I owe a special debt of gratitude to the senior leadership team of Oster Communications. Together we try to live out the principles of growth in this book. My vision has been shaped by them. My success is inextricably interwoven with theirs. What a privilege to serve with this team: Rex Wilmore, Piers Fallowfield-Cooper, Mike Walsten, Tom Noon, Merlyn VandeKrol, Karen Gleason, John Schillaci, Kurt Klein, Darrell Jobman, Jerry Carlson, Terry Wooten, Len Swiatly, Mark Wooderson, Scott Rogers, Sandy Golz, John Jokerst, John Heidersbach, Jim Wiesemeyer, Mike Klansek, Dan Manternach and our many other associates who have assisted in leading the growth process.

A thank you, also, to the Young Presidents Organization (YPO) whose universities, seminars and chapter meetings gave me an opportunity to learn in a "classroom" filled with successful "young tigers" who are willing to critique, expound, and direct based on their successes and failures in the real world. A special thanks to members of my YPO forum group which acts as a board of advisors: Larry Reed, Dennis Wood, Bill Benskin, Gary DeKoter, David Hoak, Marty Huebschman, Fred Hunt, Ken Lockard, Bill Persinger, Alan Sabbag and Tom Wenstrand.

My mother, Pearl Oster, demonstrated service to others before self to such a degree in the classroom that, to this day in the little town of New Hartford, Iowa, I am known not so much in my own right, but as "Mrs. Oster's son." My late father, Harland Oster, frequently laid aside priority work to help a neighbor shell corn, bale hay, round up a lost steer or tow a crippled vehicle. His concern for his neighbors was immense. Through my parents' efforts I saw the response of other people, the difference a steward's attitude makes in a community. During my growing up years, I saw my grandmothers, Carrie Smith and the late Bessie Oster, as people who preferred giving to taking . . . serving to being served.

No textbook or college lecture can make an impression as deep or as enduring as that of living examples in your own family.

PREFACE

My primary goal in writing this book is to paint a complete picture of the value-based, vision-driven organization with its resulting growth climate which energizes the people who make it work.

As I began my work, I sensed that a unique energy, present in nearly all businesses, can cultivate a stimulating corporate culture, *if a company places a high value on the individual and bases its action on a clear concept of fairness.* To identify the elements of success in these growing organizations, I look primarily outward at the companies started by my friends and colleagues. Occasionally I glance inward at the successes and failures of my own company.

After several years of exploration, I discovered that visionary companies create a special climate with a potent force which enables the organization's values and vision to energize and pervade and direct every corner of the operation. I call it "applied vision." In a sense, this force or creative momentum carries on and recreates entrepreneurial energy and zeal. Unleashing the learning ability and creative power of people breathes new life into a business or service organization.

FOREWORD

by Kenneth H. Blanchard, Ph.D.

Few words are bandied about and misunderstood as much as the word *vision*. For some people, it means jotting down a few lofty goals once a year and then tossing the piece of paper in a desk drawer. For others, it connotes a mystical experience that transcends everyday experience. Both miss the mark. A vision is a guiding light to live by, 365 days a year. It is the reason you go to work and the reason your organization exists. A real vision gets tucked away in the mind, not the drawer; it shapes every thought and decision.

At the same time, a vision is a spiritual statement of one's relation to God and the rest of humanity. It is this very quality that makes it so relevant to our day-to-day experience; a true vision is a blueprint for daily action.

In this book, Merrill J. Oster captures the practical aspect of vision and, in the process, introduces "applied vision." Nothing describes the purpose of true vision better than the term "applied vision." It means a culture in which an organization's highest goals infuse the whole company, so that every aspect of the operation becomes an expression of the vision. The vision, therefore, becomes evident in everything from the way the receptionist answers the phone to the way top management conducts strategic planning.

What kind of cultures support applied vision? According to Merrill, only cultures based on enduring, absolute values that uphold human dignity will guide us into the next millennium. These values are based on simple, timeless truths that make it possible to create environments free of fear . . . environments in which people can grow to their fullest potential . . . environments in which doing the right thing becomes the only option . . . environments in which people believe that service to our fellow man is the highest attainable goal. That, I believe, is what applied vision is all about.

I applaud Merrill Oster for bringing clarity to this topic in *Vision-Driven Leadership.* I hope you gain from it as much as I have.

20/20 LEADERSHIP

Companies with clear-sighted vision create a *nurturing* culture where people growth propels company growth. Visionary companies put a very high value on people, invest heavily in their training, believe in them and trust them. These companies reward people for taking a long-term, focused view in which lasting solutions to problems are sought and developed. In such cultures, there is little mention of the words "employee" and "manager." People aren't just "employees" or "human resources"; they're members of a family, associates who are empowered to use their talents in new and exciting ways.

In times of crisis, business associates are called upon to provide solutions rather than being viewed as the source of the problem and, as a result, being fired. Most important, people are encouraged to work as members of a team whose goal is to serve others—to provide total customer satisfaction.

Finally, whereas visionless cultures teach people to be satisfied with the minimum acceptable level of quality, nurturing, visionary cultures give people the freedom to strive for maximum quality—true excellence. This freedom enables them to meet the customer's ever-changing demands and needs with the highest possible quality products and services, and to enjoy the deep sense of satisfaction that comes from this high level of success.

A Question of Values

I believe that the real problems of the visionless organization culture stem from an unclear view of man. There is pressure in western society to accept a value system based on the view that man is the result of some cosmic accident. This low view of human dignity is generated by a society trying to reject a traditional value system with its roots in the belief that man is created by God, in His own image.

Historically, western society rooted its vision of the dignity of man in its Judeo-Christian belief that man is created uniquely in God's image and his chief purpose is to convey that glory as part of an eternal plan – an exalted vision of man's standing. According to this traditional view, human rights and dignity depend upon the creator who made man with dignity. In the American formulation, "men . . . are endowed by their Creator with certain inalienable rights."

In his widely read article in *Science,* "The New Biology: What Price Relieving Man's Estate?" Leon R. Kass of the University of Chicago wrote:

> We are witnessing the erosion, perhaps the final erosion, of the idea of man as something splendid or divine, and its replacement with a view that sees man, no less than nature, as simply more raw material for manipulation and homogenization.

Organizations whose leaders buy into the "scientific humanism" point of view tend to treat their employees and customers as raw material rather than as wonderfully, uniquely created beings capable of great growth and having infinite value.

Visionary cultures enable people to feel secure, knowing they have been created as unique human beings with a definite purpose. They see each person empowered with specific "gifts" to help achieve that purpose. Individuals and organizations operating with this higher vision of man operate with a clear understanding of right and wrong, based on absolute values. This approach gives people the wherewithal to see how they fit into the "big picture."

When people feel the deeper sense of belonging and purpose that should exist in the organization with the visionary, nurturing culture and traditional value system, their self-esteem rises. And with increased self-esteem, they feel confident and secure enough to take risks and assume individual responsibility.

In the pages that follow, you will be introduced to some of the people who have taken the high view of man. They treat their associates, customers and suppliers with respect. In a way, their philosophies are expressed by international real estate giant Trammel Crow's organizational chart. The top box is labeled "Customers," the middle box is labeled "People who serve customers," and, at the lowest level, the bottom box is labeled "Everybody else." Now *that's* real bottom-line thinking.

VISION AND VALUES

*A business must have a conscience
as well as a counting house.*
— Sir Montague Burton, British tailor

Living the Vision

I first met Bill Pollard as a fellow member of a board. I was struck by how he carefully used a few words to convey immense insight. His clear thinking propelled him into a highly successful career which took him to the top of ServiceMaster, one of the most consistent profit earners among service companies. Let me tell you briefly about this man I am privileged to call a friend.

When Bill faced a serious illness in his early 30s, he sensed that it was God's way of moving him from a career in corporate tax law. Teaching seemed to be his calling, so he left the corporate world and joined the faculty of Wheaton College. But his yearnings to do even more for humanity propelled him into a third career which began when he signed on as the president and CEO of Service-Master. He later became chairman of the leading supplier of hospital support services that include materials and clinical equipment maintenance, food and linen services, and home care operations. He then led the very successful billion-dollar company to diversify into school and cafeteria services, as well as commercial and residential products for lawn care, house cleaning and pest control.

For Pollard, ServiceMaster is far more than just a successful company; it is living proof that a business can be consistently run according to the principles, standards and values of the Bible. The very name "ServiceMaster" (literally, service to the Master, the Lord Jesus Christ) underscores that vision.

To fulfill the mission that its name proudly bespeaks, ServiceMaster has four objectives. The first is "To honor God in all we do."

"Our company recognizes God's sovereignty in all areas of our business. Our objective is to apply consistently the principles, standards and values of the Bible in our business attitudes and actions," Bill explains. "We believe that God has created all things and that we honor Him when we honor His creation. We do that when we create an environment in our business dealings that will help people — whether our employees or the people we serve — to become all that God has intended them to be."

The second objective is "To help people develop."

ServiceMaster boasts a comprehensive training program that ranges from basic housekeeping and technical skills to management courses equivalent to post-graduate courses. Jobs at ServiceMaster also offer exceptional upward mobility; many of the company's managers actually started off as service workers. Explains Pollard, "We believe that people grow with the challenge and opportunity for achievement that requires an individual to stretch. Employees are encouraged to expand their abilities and potential through education available outside of the company. In recruiting, developing and training employees, the company will provide an equal opportunity for all." That orientation has given ServiceMaster the reputation of being a truly caring organization.

The most important aspect of the second objective at ServiceMaster is to help people develop the servant's attitude imbued in everyone's character. "The Bible tells us, 'Whoever would be first among you, let him be your servant.' This attitude can be learned, and we communicate it through all of our training programs," says Bill. "This is a basic goal of our teaching effort."

ServiceMaster's third objective is "To pursue excellence."

Says Pollard, "We accept the responsibility to continually seek better methods to render current and new services to our customers at better value. We are committed to continue serving each of our customers with a pursuit of excellence."

The fourth and final objective is "To grow profitably."

According to Pollard, this greatly differs from the conventional approach to profit as the sole aim of being in business: "We see growth in revenue while maintaining an adequate profit both as the material means of achieving the other objectives and as a measurement of the company's value to its customers, employees and shareholders. Our company is committed to use profit with a sense of stewardship and responsibility to employees and customers while providing a means for profitable investing. In addition, we are determined to share these benefits of the free enterprise system domestically and throughout the world."

The key to ServiceMaster's success lies in the fact that its employees understand the vision of the company and have applied the four objectives in their daily work and personal lives. Citing the words of ServiceMaster's founder,

Marion Wade, Pollard says, "If you don't live it, you won't believe it. Service to the Master is a way of life."

*   *   *

The Tale of Two Cultures

Let's contrast the value-based, vision-driven culture of companies like ServiceMaster with the visionless corporate culture based on the idea that man is basically a cosmic accident, the result of chance and an evolutionary process.

The implicit message in the visionless culture is that man has no higher purpose than what is here and now; he is accountable to no higher being. He must figure out right and wrong for himself. He sees his destiny totally in his own hands. Man is the final authority, his only hope. In this setting, the value system is "whatever seems right" at the time. There are no absolutes. Many organizations try to attract and keep people based on goals of making money or advancing a career—a visionless corporate culture.

By contrast, a clear-sighted, visionary culture deeply rooted in the Judeo-Christian tradition is based on a distinctively different vision of who man is, who God is and the purpose of life. Among the tenets:

- God created every man to be unique, yet part of one body and dependent on one another;

- God considers man of inestimable value;

- God made man to be accountable and responsible, and He endowed him with the ability to attain the deep wisdom that comes from a long-term perspective;

- God made man to render service in the selfless image of the servant.

If the predominant belief in your organization is based on the former view, that man somehow materialized out of the Big Bang, then people tend to adopt the attitude that it's "every man for himself." Your organization will lack definitive reference points for determining what's right and what's wrong. You tend to depend on "situational ethics."

But if you start from the basis of the Judeo-Christian tradition, your business associates tend to act according to the belief that good work means good service to our fellow man, that right and wrong are absolute and that "long range" includes eternity. You don't have to depend exclusively on next quarter results for your satisfaction.

The lack of an absolute value system in today's typical visionless corporate culture makes it difficult to talk about ethical behavior in any meaningful way. Right and wrong can be defined in many ways in a value system based on situational ethics. Just look at the spate of indictments and convictions for insider trading that has rocked Wall Street during the past few years. The media focuses on the individual personalities and their greed. But no one has asked what it is about the cultures of these firms that make it possible for people to even *consider* such illegal and irresponsible behaviors. What is it about the culture that says it's all right for people to put their own personal gain above the trust given by their clients?

Without a set of absolute values to guide us, we slip into a kind of situational ethics system in which almost any behavior can be justified as all right "considering the situation." Nowhere is the need for a value system more evident than in the training our future captains of industry receive in business schools. In business schools today, students are typically taught that an organization has three purposes: to survive, grow and make a profit.

This shallow view of business begs the all-important

question, "Why are we in business?" Leaders must continually ask themselves this question if their companies are to grow and provide lasting value to their customers and society at large. "To survive, grow and make a profit" is no answer. None of today's great companies achieved their prominent status by operating with such a self-serving and narrow view of the world.

As my friend Bill Pollard points out, for a company to truly succeed and make a lasting mark, it must have something more than simple profitability as its driving force. Service to mankind must be central to a vision that creates sustaining energy. Profitability is a mere technical feat, and in today's ever-competitive global environment, companies must differentiate themselves by demonstrating that they truly care about their customers and their employees. They must have a leader whose vision is large enough to attract dedicated associates who want to build lasting bonds of loyalty with their customers and clients.

Let's take a closer look at the kind of people that some of today's business schools tend to churn out and contrast them with clear-sighted leaders who understand that values and vision create a growth climate that drives a business.

Valueless Vs. Value Driven

Many MBA graduates and businessmen operating under the belief that man is his own authority have some of the following elements which make up a "mindset" that siphons energy away from an organization. These men with a "scientific vision" of man:

- Believe that leadership is an inalienable right that comes with a diploma or a title.

- Have no appreciation for how companies evolve; they believe that the ability to manipulate people and money is more important than loyalty to an original idea.

- Are primarily driven by money.

- View employees as a means to an end—expendable human "resources."

- See customers as a necessary evil on the road to the highest profit, and customer service as a cloak for manipulation.

- Understand suppliers to be adversaries who can be played off against each other in a win-lose battle. Winning means hammering suppliers until they yield the lowest prices and maximum concessions, without regard for the suppliers' welfare.

- Adopt a "take no prisoners" attitude when going up against competition. They measure victory purely in terms of market share.

- Gaze into the future quarter by quarter in straight-line projections based on the current reality.

The visionary leader who sees himself as part of an eternal scene with God-created purpose in life has a very different world view and vision of his company's relationship to it. Such leaders:

- Believe that the world owes them nothing; they're here by the grace of God. Leadership is a right that has to be earned through serving in a constantly changing environment.

- Are driven by a cause. They see themselves as servants and as stewards of God-given resources. Typically, they want to improve the profits of their customers; they want to make a product or service available to little guys that had heretofore been too expensive;

they want to level the playing field so that many people can compete; they want to change the way a group of people view themselves so their communities can attain a better standard of living; and most of all, they want to achieve big, sometimes dreamy goals.

- See wealth creation in society as a means to advance the living standards of mankind, and personal wealth as a stewardship, a storehouse from which to give to others.

- View business associates as people of value who are worthy of their care and investment of time and energy. They understand that their company's growth is intrinsically linked to the nurturing and growth of their associates.

- Have a high regard for the role individual responsibility plays in personal and corporate success. Individual accountability before God forms their philosophy in the workplace.

- See customers as members of the corporate family, and customer service as a way of life.

- Understand suppliers to be an integral part of the corporate family. They take a win-win approach, because they know that their suppliers' well-being is critical to their own company's well-being.

- Avoid unnecessary head-on clashes with competitors because they believe they can find niches that complement others in the marketplace. They see competition as a healthy process that allocates resources, sharpens creativity and provides a better range of options for their customers.

- Gaze into the future by quantum leaps, starting from the current reality and moving beyond to the fulfillment of the vision.

When people approach business with these two opposing sets of attitudes, they build very different types of cultures. Those who adopt the typical business school attitudes tend to act either amorally or, worse, immorally. In contrast, visionary leaders, who act on the basis of Judeo-Christian values, take a totally ethical position, which goes beyond mere morality and sets its foundation on the timeless guidelines of biblical principles. The following section points out how the differing attitudes are manifested in the organization.

Ethical Standards

Immoral Organization: Management avoids operating within the boundaries imposed by common ethics or the law. As a result, its decisions are frequently at odds with accepted ethical and legal principles.

Moral Organization: Management operates on the basis of "contextual ethics," deciding right and wrong on a case-by-case basis. In other words, decisions are not made within an absolute moral context. The current "mores" of the day provide an ever-changing set of standards.

Ethical Organization: Management conforms to clearly understood and carefully communicated standards of right and wrong based on a value system set firmly in many absolute, God-given principles. They perform above the expected standards of their profession.

Orientation

Immoral Organization: Management is driven by greed.

Moral Organization: Management is well-intentioned, but ultimately selfish. It uses public relations to give the company the appearance of having a social conscience while it pursues self-serving goals.

Ethical Organization: Management is driven by the servant's attitude and by a desire to make a difference in the larger society.

Attitude Toward the Law

Immoral Organization: Management views the law as a barrier to be overcome or hurdled.

Moral Organization: Management goes by the letter of the law, saying, "It's okay if we can do it legally."

Ethical Organization: Management operates well above what the law mandates.

Performance Standards

Immoral Organization: Management takes a short-term view, exploiting opportunities, cutting corners and advocating the minimum level of performance that will keep customers happy.

Moral Organization: Driven by a philosophy of what is the "least we can offer" to satisfy the needs of the highest possible profit within the guidelines of what seems right in today's society.

Ethical Organization: Management upholds customer satisfaction as the highest possible goal, frequently at a cost to the company in the short run.

Interpersonal Relations

Immoral Organization: Management promotes distrust for others and encourages people to focus on the corporate ladder. People are rewarded for back-stabbing and finger-pointing as they clamor for the next rung.

Moral Organization: Management sends vague messages regarding proper behavior to the rest of the company because it operates with a floating value system. People are left to their own devices to guess whether or not a certain behavior toward their fellow employees is acceptable.

Ethical Organization: Management sends a clear message regarding expected behavior, and creates an environment based on openness, honesty and trust. People have a sense of belonging, as in a family.

Response to Breeches of Ethics and Public Liability

Immoral Organization: Management stonewalls by denying its responsibility or attempts a cover-up.

Moral Organization: Management ignores the situation hoping it will go away. Action is only taken if social pressure or the long arm of the law is brought to bear.

Ethical Organization: Management opens its doors and admits its mistakes, willfully making restitution where applicable and asking forgiveness from the associates within the company and the community at large.

Attitudes Toward Accountability

Immoral Organization: Management sees itself as accountable to no one.

Moral Organization: Management has a sense of social and professional responsibility, but does little to go beyond what is expected.

Ethical Organization: Management holds itself to a set of philosophical standards rooted in ageless principles, and regards itself as accountable to a higher being.

At this point, after reading through the list of totally ethical characteristics, you might ask if companies can really succeed in upholding them all the time. The fact is, thousands of small and large companies live by these principles. They are led by people with a commitment to vision and values. They see beyond wealth for wealth's sake.

Yes, there are companies and organizations in our world that will fight accountability to the bitter end. But then there are ethical companies like Johnson & Johnson that survive a major product liability crisis and emerge as heroes.

Rather than stonewalling when six people died after taking cyanide-tainted extra-strength Tylenol capsules, J&J's leaders flung open the boardroom doors during daily emergency meetings and invited the media. J&J also shook the industry by taking the unprecedented action of voluntarily pulling all extra-strength Tylenol from the nation's shelves at a loss of $100 million. The company then instituted new triple protection wrapping before the government mandated such steps. This was all the more commendable given the fact that Johnson & Johnson was the victim of a madman's whim and had not done anything harmful itself. Because of its honest actions, J&J saved its good name, and within a year Tylenol had recovered nearly 80 percent of its previous market share.

Another large firm, Caterpillar Tractor Company, also set a standard for big business by developing a manual that would help its sales reps do business in international settings where bribery and other unethical behaviors are commonplace. The manual clearly spells out how to carry on negotiations without compromising the company's highest standards of ethics.

And W. L. Gore demonstrated a visionary sense when it dismantled the corporate ladder in favor of an environment where each individual rises to his or her highest level of ability and is compensated with no regard to hierarchy. This approach eliminates the kind of petty infighting for position that pits colleague against colleague at the expense of productivity and overall performance.

Finally, the Fortune 500 and 1000 lists contain many companies that recognize the importance of "stakeholders" — employees, suppliers, people in the surrounding community. IBM, for example, allows certain levels of management to take a sabbatical and give something back to the surrounding community.

In one project, an IBM manager set up an herb greenhouse in the South Bronx. The project, partially owned by IBM's local employees, took off as New York's finest restaurants clamored for the fresh herbs being grown across town. In a way, the project was too successful; the IBMer left his company to work on the greenhouse full time, hoping to help other economically depressed areas take advantage of abandoned space.

McDonald's, Hines and other major corporations are also known for their generous corporate philanthropy and social responsibility, further proving that a vision based on serving one's fellow man can prevail in a company regardless of size or industry.

The Benefits of Mixing Values and Business

Leaders who are vision-driven don't need inducements for operating in an ethical manner. They know that the most important benefit of operating from a base of a changeless value system is a tremendous improvement in efficiency. If you know the boundaries, you don't waste time and energy worrying about what's right and what's wrong. You instinctively sort right from wrong.

You also develop a reputation as being trustworthy, which in business is a priceless asset. If people believe in you, you can operate on the basis of your word, crossing the "T's" later.

A related benefit is that companies with a reputation for high ethical standards attract highly ethical people who know what constitutes acceptable behavior. For example, they know that there's no need to engage in corporate espionage to gain a competitive edge. They understand that the best information about the competition comes from reading the business press and listening to their salespeople and customers. In short, they know that all the information they need to get ahead is in the library or on the street.

Ethical management also results in better customer service because it attracts people who will go the extra mile for the customer. These people go far beyond the nine-to-five mentality that leaves customers in need hanging from

5:01 on Friday until 9:01 on Monday morning. People in value-driven companies know they are empowered to use their creativity to its fullest potential to help customers. And they do.

In addition to enjoying the benefits of employees who care about customers, companies that are driven by a clear-cut set of values offer higher quality products and services. Their employees know that quality is a lifetime effort, and that attention to details, along with the relentless pursuit of the elimination of waste, makes the company stronger and gives it the ultimate competitive advantage.

Value-based companies also reap the benefits of win-win relations with vendors. They may not get the absolute rock-bottom price on supplies, materials and parts, but they can count on vendors who will stick with them through thick and thin, helping them solve problems and develop new products and services.

Another benefit of operating from a clearly-defined value base is that little time, energy and money is spent fighting head-to-head battles with competitors. Value-based companies avoid mutually destructive battles for minuscule gains in market share. Rather, they capitalize on their strengths and do a better job of filling a market niche.

Finally, companies based on timeless values can cope with the sometimes fickle winds of change. Timeless values are not jarred by new players in the global marketplace, fluctuations in exchange rates, the introduction of new technologies and other inevitable events that every business will experience in the decade to come. And in the long run, organizations that can easily adapt to such forces will become the vanguard companies of the new millennium.

Obviously, there are many fine companies operating at a very high level of caring for their employees which subscribe to the "scientific vision" of man as a cosmic accident with no higher purpose than serving himself here and now. Likewise, there are companies whose leadership holds to a higher view of man, but treats customers and associates poorly. Over time, however, the company whose leadership is set on treating people well, based on the high view of man, will tend to create an atmosphere where individuals grow and where their individual growth fuels the organization's growth.

Here are the basic core values we act upon in our publishing company:

OSTER COMMUNICATIONS, INC.

VALUES STATEMENT

A value-based organization creates a nurturing, visionary climate.

Result: Success. Individual and corporate growth through the continual achievement of worthy goals which leads organizations toward fulfillment of their missions.

SOME CORE VALUES...	AND THE MESSAGES A NURTURING, VISIONARY CLIMATE SENDS ITS PEOPLE BY ACTIONS BASED ON THESE VALUES
We are created with a purpose.	"We believe that you are a created being of infinite value. Our creator has a plan for each of us. You are important to Him and to us."
We grow by exercising our unique gifts.	"In this organization you are expected to use your gifts and talents and watch them develop. Our organization growth depends on your growth."
We are part of a team.	"Your family team and relationships are important to us. Our organization

is another family where we work together and encourage each other as we achieve common goals. No one goes it alone in this organization. We need each other."

We are individually responsible.

"Team members hold themselves accountable for specific areas of performance and do not point the finger at other teams or individuals to cover for their personal shortcomings. As each individual enlarges his area of personal responsibility, we grow."

The truth sets us free.

"Please tell it straight to us, our customers and suppliers. Deception in any form inhibits our growth because it removes the important element of mutual trust. But the truth spoken harshly can hurt, so speak the truth in love. An accurate assessment of our current situation is a vital base for realizing our goals."

Selflessness frees us to serve.

"We are here to serve others — our customers as well as others in the organization. Stealing, cheating, 'personal empire building' or other self-serving activities only detract from our growth. As we surrender our 'rights,' we gain ultimate effectiveness. Generosity is a lubricant which frees our spirit and helps us grow."

Love goes beyond fairness.

"Love goes beyond doing the expected. Love sacrifices its personal interest to advance the cause of others. This attitude toward each other, our customers and our suppliers energizes us and gives us an identity. We are judged by how we show our love."

Occasional pruning promotes new growth.

"We must look for ways to most efficiently use our limited resources. That means we need your help in spotting activities which generate negative results. Even those activities that generate good results but aren't central to our mission must be eliminated. A growth climate is one of gradual change and continual improvement."

Excellence adds distinctive value.

"We can't be just another provider of a generic service. Through the pursuit of excellence, our products must be the best in their niche. We can do this only if you become the best possible person you can be. Products and service follow."

Wealth creators serve society.

"Proper conservation and use of our time and money help us generate profitable results. Only the organizations which earn more than they spend can pay taxes, give and, in various other ways, make a contribution to society. We fight poverty in our community by creating employment opportunities and investing a portion of our earnings in worthy causes."

Forgiveness erases mistakes.

"You will make mistakes; so will we. Let's learn to forgive so we create an atmosphere where people are willing to take a chance to risk failure in the pursuit of finding new and better ways to serve. Failure is only temporary. It is a learning experience. We

	must take risks to find continual improvement. Promoting the status quo, although seemingly safe, stifles growth."
Optimism hastens growth.	"There is hope of victory both for mankind in general and for us in the pursuit of our specific goals. We have positive expectations for you and reinforce those expectations by celebrating our victories."
Vision guides and energizes.	"We want you to know where the organization is headed. We want your input in reshaping our vision corporately and team by team. Communication with your team leader and team members is vital so you are energized by knowing how your efforts fit into the team and organizational vision."

*   *   *

HANDS ON

Value Check

Sometimes the best way to stimulate a discussion of values and ethics is to pose a difficult situation that falls in the grey area and ask people to comment on it. The following scenario, which was developed by Leonard Fuld, president of Information Data Search and one of the nation's leading experts on competitor intelligence, can help you do just that.

Ask your managers to read the scenario and develop positions. Then ask them to use it in discussions with their teams or divisions. More important than specific solutions to the dilemma are the values and ethical standards that are sure to be articulated during the discussions. You can then use the discussions as a starting point for identifying areas of strength and weakness in your company's value system.

The Scenario

Imagine that a product manager of your company is visiting a printer to get an estimate for a brochure about a new line. While he's there, he glances down at the end of the counter and can't help but notice the proof for a brochure from a competitor. The information gained would give your company a tremendous edge in positioning its new product. Clearly, the information was obtained by accident rather than by willful breach of the law or standards of professional conduct. But is it ethical for your company to use it before the information is public knowledge?

THE BIRTH
OF A VISION

*Make no little plans. There is nothing in little
plans that stirs men's blood. Make big plans.
Once a big idea is recorded it can never die.*
— Daniel Burnham, Chicago Plan Commission

Stepping Into a Dream

I sat riveted to my chair in an Atlanta restaurant,
listening to a quietly confident presentation of an idea that
could revolutionize the way companies train their associates. This was my first meeting with Bill Schwarz
whose start-up company went from one capital shortage to
another without dimming the founder's vision.

Bill Schwarz has been a teacher and entrepreneur all
his adult life, although not in the conventional sense. For
twenty years he owned and operated a company committed
to promoting meaningful organizational change. Learning
Laboratories, Inc., provided training in leadership and
organization change to corporations throughout the
United States. Then at age forty, Bill asked himself, "What
one idea is worth dedicating the next forty years of my life
to achieve?"

After pondering the question, a notion began to churn in his head, an idea for the ultimate way of helping people grow in corporate environments so their companies could become world-class organizations. The result: Corporate Satellite Television Network, Inc. (CSTN). With CSTN, companies committed to a vision of organizational excellence would have the ability to implement and execute their plan with a consistent, continuous improvement process.

The CSTN commitment to clients is a minimum of three to five years of delivering a customized training curriculum via satellite television. Sessions would be designed for all levels of management and every employee on a work team. They would be taught by experts in organizational excellence, all part of a "faculty" of master teachers and leading-edge thinkers.

After five years of following a well-designed plan of five phases and meeting seemingly endless disappointments, including totally impossible situations that required Schwarz and his wife Laurie to invest everything they had ever possessed, CSTN finally had all of its systems and people in place, and began its first educational offerings in 1989.

"Our company was one of the first to train its associates on team building, quality improvement and customer service via the network," says Bill. "We've had great results."

It was a long, hard road for Bill, but his persistence and faith in the value of what he had dedicated himself to doing for the rest of his life had given birth to an innovative company. One reason we became friends is that we both survived start-up years when a few folks thought we'd never make it. Our dedication to a vision pulled us through.

"When the idea first began percolating in my head," Bill recalls, "I didn't sleep for days. I wrote, did research and introduced myself to entirely new communities of people. I also knew I could try to fund this in one of two ways. One way was to continue my existing business and use it to support the new project. But I realized that the existing business would demand too much energy because of the level of commitment every current or future client required. I knew I'd be on a treadmill with my energy in two places. So I fulfilled my current commitments and set out with my vision."

The second way, says Bill, was to fund the plan through venture capital: "I figured it would take $12 million, and to raise that kind of money would definitely result in entrusting the dream to the financial interests of others. Investors and venture capitalists who were interested in CSTN seemed more concerned about protecting their interests than ensuring CSTN's success. That attitude stifles your energy.

"So if a process does not release energy and breathe life into it and all those associated with it, abandon it and move on. It was then that I discovered that to succeed, you must make the dream real by just stepping out and taking action. Each step creates the next one."

For Bill, leaping into the unknown was essential to transforming the dream into a reality. "When you step out of the dream and begin taking action, you've succeeded. Maybe not in terms of the eventual goals, but in a nonlinear way, you've done it," he says. "When you step into absolute uncertainty, you also open yourself up for limitless resources. All that sounds good in theory, but in practice, it's *incredible*! It goes beyond your wildest dreams. One thing just leads to another; every time a door closes, you discover others that you could not see before. That's because when you become dependent on something, it becomes a block to the creative process—you drain the life out of it. So every time someone says no or something sours, you must be grateful, thank them and step out again from limited to limitless resources."

On the surface, many things that looked like lifelines for CSTN turned out to be quicksand pits. And many things that looked like they were negatives turned out to be the lifesavers.

"For example, we had several opportunities for joint ventures," Bill explains. "Each time, these looked like what we needed to really get rolling. The partners could provide the TV studios and equipment we needed. It turned out that they didn't share our vision, lacked a vision of their own or that they wanted us to be short-term solutions to *their* problems. In that way, *we* would become a deficit to them.

"We learned quickly that for others to help us realize our dream, there had to be exceptional synergy. Our cultures and staff had to mesh perfectly and create something in which the whole was greater than the sum of the parts. So, time and again, we were back on our own, investing our thinking in the creative process and trying to forge ahead."

Today, Bill Schwarz has finally found partnering arrangements in which everyone retains their autonomy, but they've also identified common ways that they can build something greater for all involved. "One of the secrets to such partnership," Schwarz insists, "is to be totally truthful. If you're broke, tell 'em you're broke. Lay it out in the rawest fashion, because your partners will eventually find out, and the instant they sense that they're being told a story, it's over. As soon as a little doubt gets into the dream it's like a cancer that spreads."

To manage the dream, Bill says, you must keep looking at everything that's happening as *data,* not good or bad. Never get caught thinking something is good or bad. Once the dream is there, everything that goes on in life serves it one way or another. Schwarz reminds us that "Jesus said, 'Let those who have eyes to see . . . see.' I think He meant that once you have a dream, you'll have eyes to see what others are blind to. I came to realize that everything I see, every person I meet, is part of the dream. If I can't make a mortgage payment, that's serving the dream—it means that I have to discover a whole new set of resources.

"I have to be open, truthful and honest in new ways. If I can make all my payments, have all of the required resources, what's the big deal? No real need to discover new paradigms. You have to go to a whole other level of saying, 'Am I committed to the dream? Am I willing to risk my house and cause my family to live in uncertainty?' You have to talk to yourself and your family in a whole new way. You create a new set of relationships with all of your old relationships."

In short, Bill believes that starting a new company is a spiritual journey. "A lot of people talk about having faith. They believe that they have it, yet they are still full of fear. They do not want uncertainty. With faith there is *only* uncertainty, but there are levels of faith," he says. "The only thing you can see in this world is yourself reflected everywhere. If I'm truly one who is serving others, and my dream is committed to serving others, then all I can see is everything serving me and the dream. So to have eyes that see, I must truly know who I am. If I see everything going on in my life as serving the dream and myself as its steward, then I have a purpose. But I don't have a purpose if I see things as obstacles or blocks; the instant that happens the dream is gone, replaced by misperceptions of reality and barriers."

For Bill, the world keeps revealing what is concealed, dictating what you have to give next in order to receive. It's very close up and personal. It is always opening up, not closing up. Even if something seems like a speck or a nuance, he urges everyone to stop and look at it, for even the tiniest little thing may be an entirely new universe. "Above all," he says, "if you nurture the dream you won't give in to fear. You must keep walking one step at a time. Those who do so will transform cultures and set nations free."

★   ★   ★

The Core Idea

The visionary idea is the leading force behind any business. While the vision itself may result in a complex or sophisticated product or service, in most cases the core idea is a simple one.

For Bill Schwarz, the idea was a new, economical way to help give corporations the real tools they needed to bring about lasting organizational change, change that leads to better customer service and more satisfied associates. In the case of Oster Communications, the idea was to first create a newsletter that would help farm families earn a profit by using futures markets and current knowledge to better manage risk. That vision at Oster later expanded to include businessmen in general, by showing them how to manage risks that could be hedged in futures markets. And in the case of ServiceMaster, the idea was to build a service company that is led by people who love growth.

Where do such visionary ideas originate? How do you get them? These questions are really equivalent to asking: "How do you think creatively?" Sadly, no subject has engendered more mental chicanery and nonsense than creativity. Today, so-called creativity experts and consultants prance about corporate boardrooms and seminar halls like sword-swallowing magicians, goading people into performing mental gymnastics that might be amusing, but in fact have nothing to do with helping them think more creatively.

The best thing anyone can do is point out both the subtle barriers and obvious roadblocks that prevent many people from unleashing their God-given powers of innovative thinking. This chapter is designed to show you ways to open your mind to your own creative energy. It is aimed at unleashing the wealth of fresh thinking that may lead to a dramatic new vision for yourself, your family or your business.

Opening Your Mind

The creative mind is like a parachute — it works only when it's open. When you're experimenting with visionary ideas, *anything* is fair game initially. As soon as you begin thinking, "Well, that's ridiculous . . . that's impractical . . . that's impossible," you end your personal brainstorming session and shut off the flow of creative ideas. Sure, all ideas must at some point pass a reality check, and many, if not most, won't be feasible in the long run. But to distill those few truly creative ideas that can redirect your business in a new direction, launch a new product or service, or even spawn a whole new company or industry, you must refrain from dropping the hammer too quickly and dismissing an idea as outlandish.

Think of all the wonderful companies and products that would never have come to pass if someone hadn't said, "Hey, wait a minute. Don't discard that idea. It's a winner." Consider the story of a "failed" glue experiment at 3M. The new glue was tossed into the trash can because it didn't stick. After all, what good is a glue that won't hold things together?

It's very good, discovered 3M scientist Art Fry, when you need to stick something on a piece of paper temporarily. Like a book marker. At the time of the experiment, Fry was coincidentally looking for a better book mark. He sang in his church choir and was constantly frustrated by all the little scraps of paper falling out of his hymn book.

One evening while daydreaming, his mind turned to the failed glue and he made the connection between the glue that didn't stick and the better book mark. When he made up a pad of the slightly sticky pieces of paper, he knew that he had done more than solve an age-old problem—he had created a new product with enormous sales potential for his company. And right he was!

Post-It notes, as the product was later dubbed, quickly turned into a $100 million a year item, as well as a solution to the hymn book problem.

One can find similar stories in almost all industries, where an apparent flop turns out to be the key to an immensely successful product or business. The same holds for visionary ideas; don't dismiss what may seem to be just a pipe dream, something unattainable. If your vision is to create an entity that provides the ultimate in customer service, then don't settle for less!

Everyone you read about in this book had a vision that could be dismissed as "unattainable" because of the limitations of human nature. But they held on to their goals and then began finding the means to make them happen. Patience. Foresight. Boundless vision. These are the qualities that turn managers into leaders and dreams into reality.

Where Do Creative Business Ideas Come From?

Throughout our schooling we're continually taught to think analytically. We're taught to "analyze" a piece of literature, to frame a scientific problem or to interpret an historical event. Where in this process do we learn to nurture our intuitive selves, our feeling selves? Nowhere, unfortunately; if anything, we're taught to distrust our intuitive side.

Certainly, analytical thinking is important for success in business today. But it is only part of that success. If analysis were the whole game, then most businesses could be run by computers. The fact is, intuition is a critical success factor. The best entrepreneurs and CEOs rely heavily on a keen understanding of some marketplace, some technology, and on their intuitive sense of what will fly, what won't, what's worth taking a gamble on and what's just a bad risk. In other words, they trust their hunches. They are able to see things in a different light than other people see them.

Some experts believe that creativity is essentially an articulation of the intuitive spirit. Allow yourself to respond from the gut—you can always shape or reject an idea later once you get it on the drawing board.

Above all, don't try too hard. You can't make a creative thought happen by sheer willpower. Take a cue from the ancient Chinese philosopher, Mencius, who wrote about a farmer who thought he could make his crops grow quicker by pulling on them. In the end, the farmer was left with a pile of dead plants and nothing to show for the season. The same is true of a visionary idea. If you try and force it to germinate, your labor will probably bear little fruit.

The Purpose of the Dream

According to conventional textbook wisdom, you create a mission statement, then build a company around it.

In reality, mission statements rarely guide the entrepreneur. They are, instead, used to guide others to a common understanding of the "big picture," the "big opportunity." But what happens to the *idea* in its infancy?

Where does it come from? Not from the mission statement, and certainly not through a business planning process. The fact is, the idea for a new business (or a new product or service, for that matter) emerges from a non-logical plane of reality governed by intuition or insight, not rationality.

Evaluating a Dream

All potentially successful business ideas are rooted in a single principle: the will to serve our fellow man. As Peter Drucker, the famed management expert, puts it, "Business is about attracting customers . . . creating value they can't find elsewhere."

Even the best ideas, though, may ultimately wither if they aren't properly nurtured in an entrepreneurial "hothouse." Many seeds of ideas get buried in the process of developing a business plan, attracting people and attracting money. Those that ultimately reach fruition are constantly nurtured through the gentle but constant questioning of the entrepreneur, who must ask questions such as:

1. How would the idea benefit the customer?

2. How is it better than other ideas or services already on the market?

3. What is the market potential—three thousand or three million?

4. Is it defendable—will it be easily cloned or does it present a unique twist?

5. Can you get other people to begin to buy into the idea and work alongside you during the early critical days?

Ask yourself these questions and pose them to others, too. Successful entrepreneurs use other people as reality checks and sounding boards. They intuitively separate negativism from constructive challenges and criticisms. The former emanates from a knee-jerk reaction to anything new:

"It can't work because we've never done it."

"400,000 new businesses start every year and 350,000 fail. Why become a statistic?"

Murphy's Law: "If anything can go wrong it will."

Constructive criticism, on the other hand, bolsters an idea by focusing your attention on weak spots and reinforcing the idea's strengths. This is crucial, because at a certain point in the idea development or dream process, you'll begin "talking to mirrors"; that is, you'll lose all objectivity regarding the merit of your idea and its long-term viability.

I'll never forget the war in my mind as I formulated my first publication idea. I had a good understanding of what made an agribusinessman tick because I grew up as one and spent seven years traveling the nation as a young journalist asking them about their successes. When I ran my newsletter idea by these potential customers, I got a good response.

I wanted the letters to go first-class mail (there was little, if any, agribusiness management information or market news and analysis available in a timely fashion in 1972). I wanted to talk about futures markets, using the terminology of the world's grain merchants. But the economic reality meant that if I were to attract a top flight staff to such a quality publication, I would have to charge at least $50 per year and hope for 1,000 customers to break even.

When I posed that probability to fellow journalists and publishers, they thought I was crazy to risk my life savings on such an idea. But I kept talking to the potential customers about the idea, enlarging the newsletter idea to include a package of services: membership meetings, travel, group discounts on certain purchases. These ideas weren't totally unique. I had some experience marketing a related concept for soybean growers, and some as an employee of another newsletter organization. Pieces of my dream were based on real-world experiences.

But the real conviction in my own heart came when potential end users continued to encourage me, even though the professionals were naysayers.

In 1973, I attracted long-time friend Jerry Carlson to move from Philadelphia to Cedar Falls, Iowa, to help give birth to Professional Farmers of America. We attracted 1,000 members the first year, and doubled every year until we reached 30,000 members. This initial newsletter success became the base for a company which has started or acquired forty-eight small products or companies, some of which have global reach today.

We still "baby" new ideas and new projects — treating them like little chicks that must be handled with extreme care. The forces of organizations and a busy world can more easily kill than create good ideas.

Opening the Dream to Others

At some point, the idea needs to be committed to paper, not necessarily in the form of a formalized business plan, but in a way that expresses the idea so that others can test it in their thinking, shape it and help direct it to a test.

Start by scratching out your idea on the back of an envelope or on a napkin. Some early advertisements for Compaq computers claim that the founders sat down and actually used a napkin to sketch out a better computer. Whether or not the story is true, Compaq certainly did rise to become one of the greatest success stories in recent business history.

Your "mini-mission statement" can be used to spark enthusiasm in others. You'll be able to instantly tell whether the idea clicks with someone: Either his eyes will sparkle, showing you've struck a "responsive chord," or they'll glaze over, indicating that the idea didn't connect, isn't clear or doesn't interest him.

In the idea development process you will need to attract two or three people to actually get the business to the next level of existence. They form your "brain trust." Maybe these people will be part-timers; maybe they'll be joining you on a "sweat equity" basis. Maybe they will be coaches or advisors, possibly full partners.

Whatever arrangements you make, this band of people will begin to expand your vision. They must test and retest your idea, "bullet-proofing" it from all angles and ensuring its worthiness. Moreover, if you need funding, your core group will have to pull together the documentation or prototype you need to convince investors, bankers or venture capitalists.

In addition to surrounding yourself with a dedicated band of people, you should begin to bring in high level advisors who can help your idea take shape.

Bear in mind that these are people who can help you, not control you. Their function is to challenge you in healthy ways. Even as the business matures, you can maintain an imaginary advisory board to help you make difficult decisions. Make a mental phone call to each member of the board and look for a nay or a yea on tough issues. In this way, you can perform a quick decision "audit" without leaving your office. Of course, while this technique is good for giving you an extra boost in confidence, there's no substitute for a roomful of experts eager to lend their opinion on weighty issues.

At this point in the process, you've nurtured an idea for a new business or one for revitalizing an old business. You've shared it with others who have helped to push the idea from the twilight dream state to edges of reality. In the next chapter, we'll explore how an idea gets rooted in reality through the process of creating a clear-sighted mission statement that serves as a beacon for your enterprise.

*   *   *

HANDS ON

Dreaming Your Way to Reality

When you put this book down, take out a pencil and piece of paper and imagine a much-needed product or service. Whether it's a better mousetrap, a better newsletter or a better way of managing money, think about how *you* could fulfill that dream. If your present company has the legs to deliver the product or service, visualize how the resources around you could be redeployed. If you're an entrepreneur, think about how you could build an entire company around the creation and delivery of the goods.

Perhaps writing an actual script would be helpful. Create the script as if you were writing a play. Think about the plot and identify the main characters. As you read your script, let your mind's eye develop the themes and the people until they're old friends.

Remember Bill Schwarz's comment: *Once you step into the dream, you've succeeded.* Perhaps this will be the start of a bold new venture, one that takes your present company or a new company on a journey that culminates with a product or service that improves the quality of life of your fellow man.

THE BIRTH
OF A MISSION

*To be more than a slothful steward of the talents
given in his keeping, the executive has to accept
responsibility for making the future happen. It is
the willingness to tackle purposefully this, the last
of the economic tasks in business enterprise, that
distinguishes the great business from the merely
competent one, and the business builder from the
executive-suite custodian.*

—Peter F. Drucker, **Managing for Results**

A Man Possessed by His Vision

Bob Denckhoff is an enthusiastic leader whom I met
at an area officers' meeting of the Young Presidents Organization. He has taken the idea of "mission" out of the
clouds and has shown me how a clear, people-related mission can be a potent leading force in a growing company. In
Bob's case, he used it to revitalize an existing company.
Listen in and catch his spirit.

"About eleven years ago," recalls Bob Denckhoff,
president of Missouri Encom, Inc., "I took a look at our
company and asked myself, 'If I did nothing to make it

change and let it go another ten years, would I like what I'd see?' " The answer, he says, was a flat no.

The reason? The envelope business was fraught with competitors, and his company had difficulty in differentiating itself. In 1933, when Denckhoff's father started the business, there was more demand than supply. "A fella could 'niche' himself nicely," Denckhoff says wistfully. "But technology revolutionized the industry and more players came in, glutting the market."

There was another reason for Denckhoff's discontent. "I have a passion for the person," he explains. "I want to help people totally succeed. For me, that means getting involved with a client's strategic direction and supplying him with a single product that solves all his marketing needs. Envelopes just didn't do that for me. I wanted to give people complete direct mail services, from A to Z."

The most serious problem for Denckhoff, though, was the quality of the business he was running. The attitude and values of some of the people in his shop were simply not in tune with his own. Denckhoff knew that he wanted a company with a special vision, a company whose people cared for and loved each other and their customers. In short, Denckhoff wanted to create a family of people brought together by a common desire to serve in the most humble of ways.

Once Denckhoff knew where he wanted to go strategically (a total direct mail service in which envelope production was but one small piece) and spiritually (a company based on love and trust both inside and outside its walls), he took his top people offsite and tried to bring about a new way of thinking. "We took a look at the organization, the economic environment, and put together a mission statement," recounts Denckhoff. "That meant more than writing down an idea and filing it. For us, the mission wasn't seen as a destination, but was understood to be a journey that would allow us to constantly revisit and reaffirm our vision."

To make his vision work, Denckhoff knew he must have the right people: "I believe I can be successful and achieve my goals to the extent that my people's lives are in order and that we share common priorities and values. So I earnestly seek out people who think as I do, who have similar morals and values. I let people know where we stand on the family. I want them to know that when they're hurting we care for them—that's first. This allows us to develop an *esprit* and unity that you can't put a price on."

How does Denckhoff find the kind of employees he's seeking? "You don't necessarily have to hire folks who have been in the industry; more important, you hire folks who *care.* As long as they care you can teach them the job skills. If they don't have a caring view, you can't change them and you'll never be confident that when you leave, the second shift will do its work."

Through normal attrition and replacement over the past decade, coupled with "ruthless hiring" practices, Denckhoff has surrounded himself with the kind of people he knows will do the job in the most caring way. "I'm just starting to see the fruits of my labor," he asserts with pride. "I've got guys and gals who sit at the top of the company and they care. They have high energy and run a fast race, and even more important, they understand that customers are part of our family. It's incredibly successful and satisfying to know that this company really cares about my relationship with my wife, with my kids; and everyone else knows that I care about their relationships, too."

Sometimes people look at Denckhoff's 150-member family and ask to see his corporate handbook. After all, it must contain some remarkable text to get people to perform with such vigor and dedication. When this happens, Denckhoff quietly laughs and opens the top drawer of his desk. "Oh, we do have a 'corporate handbook,' all right. It's called the Bible. Cover to cover, it's the most marvelous management strategy ever written. Look to the Book of Proverbs. Look what's spelled out. Everything you need is right there."

Reminiscing about his moment of truth ten years ago when he charted a new course for Missouri Encom, Denckhoff sums up his life: "I'm a man possessed by his vision. I'm grateful and humbled by it. I am simply a servant who has been blessed with the chance to watch a metamorphosis being created according to God's plan for the marketplace."

*   *   *

Anatomy of a Mission

Bob Denckhoff's vision created an organization that treated its own people and customers as an extended family and created a loving and caring environment in which everyone prospered spiritually as well as materially. That's his secret to adding value to differentiate himself from other generic products and services.

The strategy for making the dream come true was a revitalized company geared toward one-stop shopping for the customer, a company of caring people that could offer total service. The tactic was a reorganization combined with "ruthless hiring" techniques that brought in the kind of employees who shared Denckhoff's sense of purpose and value.

At some point, you will need to write down a mission statement. Again, this is not an exercise that you do once and then continue functioning as you had in the past. Nor is it something that you do once and then revisit annually. Writing a mission statement is a dynamic action, involving those who must make it happen. The result is a document that helps you take the pulse of your company over time.

The mission statement keeps people moving in the same direction every day. In as simple a form as possible, it captures the reason that the business exists. As the underlying vision becomes better developed, the mission statement should change. As the company develops more effective ways to fulfill the mission, the mission statement will change. And as the company finds new niches and new ways to serve humankind, the mission statement will change. Nevertheless, the vision underlying the mission statement, if it is truly clear-sighted, will remain constant throughout the evolution of the company. In this way, a mission statement represents both a "slice in time" as well as a stepping-stone in an ongoing line of thought.

Here's an example of a mission statement from Beeba's Creations Incorporated, a highly successful women's clothing manufacturer. They've dedicated themselves to filling a niche by ever drawing on its strengths as a major manufacturer (see chapter 9 for more details about this company):

> To be a major wholesaler of large quantities of a wide assortment of garments, mostly women's sportswear and related items, at low price points and reliable quality. To be an important resource for large retailers through timely delivery of goods that sell well as a result of our excellence in product development and merchandising. To excel at minimizing the production cycle time. To assist retailers by providing responsible services that help them meet their goals successfully. To minimize inventory risk by emphasizing pre-sold goods. To maximize shareholder value by developing distinct and lasting competitive advantages and achieving above-average returns. To follow the Golden Rule in all our business activities and relationships.

As you can see, this statement says it all—the *ration-*

ale for doing business entwined with a *philosophy* of doing business. Each company will have its own unique rationale, depending on its industry, product lines, etc. The philosophy of doing business will flow from a deep analysis of your beliefs about people and your purpose on this earth. The rest of this chapter provides a framework for conducting a "mission analysis" in your firm.

Framing Your Mission

The process of framing or reframing a mission entails answering the two basic questions that shape any workable vision: Where are we today? Where do we want to be at some specific date in the future? This simple act inspired Bob Denckhoff to see his company in a new light and develop a plan for revitalizing it. You, too, can use the technique to achieve dramatic results with your own business.

Here are some things to think about when you ponder the questions for yourself:

Where Are We Today?

When assessing the present status of your company, look beyond the bottom line and ask:

- If I were a customer of my own company, would I be totally loyal or would I consider going to a competitor for better quality or service?

- If I were an employee of my own company, would I feel like I'm part of a family that really cares about me?

- Is the environment in my company one of teamwork or internal wrangling and jockeying for position?

- How is success measured and rewarded in my company? Does anyone ever get a pat on the back for doing things right?

- Are people encouraged to use and develop their minds on the job?

- How quickly do we respond to change in the marketplace?

Where Do We Want to Be in Five Years, Ten Years?

- Given the company's present environment, what will it be like to work here a decade from now?

- Is our product line flexible to meet changing customer needs?

- As competitive pressures increase, will we be able to offer the same level of quality or would we have to cut corners to survive?

- Will this company have made a contribution to the world in five or ten years, or will it exist merely to sustain itself?

Developing a Mission Strategy

Once you answer questions like the above, a statement of your company's big vision is easier to narrow down into a sentence or short paragraph. Then you are ready to develop a strategy for change. Perhaps you'll discover that your organization is indeed staffed by the kind of caring people who function as a family. But despite that tremendously advantageous situation, the company just can't respond quickly enough to change to make it a long-term success. Your strategy, then, might be to build in more flexibility through improved technology and education.

The converse might also be true: Your company has the technological wherewithal to meet customers' needs under any circumstances, but because of a genuine lack of caring on the part of the employees, quality is sometimes erratic and ship dates are missed. Your strategy would be to instill a quality perspective in your employees and to get them to understand that customers are really part of the same team, not just faces on the other side of the counter.

The possible business strategy scenarios are virtually limitless. Whatever strategy you develop for your business, the key to its success is converting the vision into reality by devising and applying tactics that work effectively.

Developing Mission Tactics

Tactics allow you to test a strategy and put it to work. A strategy without tactics is just a wish. A tactic might be a reorganization of a division or the entire company. It might entail the development of a new product line or the deletion of an old one. It might involve the creation of a new department so the company can provide better service to customers. Or it might involve a new incentive or reward system.

Of course, the specific tactics you choose will depend on the nature of your business and the problems you're trying to resolve. Nevertheless, the following kinds of questions will help you determine what kind of tactics are appropriate for the task you're facing. As you answer these questions you begin to shape the tactical plans which relate to specific areas of your business.

People:

- Do you have the right kind of people in your organization? Can you define what "right" means for you?

- What kind of incentives would be required to get your people to share your vision for the company?

- Would some of your associates be better off elsewhere and, if so, how could you help relocate them?

Culture:

- Is your culture conducive to doing business in the fashion you desire?

- If your culture doesn't fit your vision, what kinds of changes need to be made?

- How should change be introduced in your company?

- Can your culture withstand a major change?

- How can your culture foster innovation and creative thinking if it doesn't already?

- If you had the luxury of starting from scratch, how would you build a company? How can you transplant that framework onto your existing company?

Products:

- Do your existing products and service meet your standards? Even if they do, how can you raise the "high bar" and add more value?

- Can you see your products and services being of value in the next five years? The next ten years?

Resources:

- Do you have the financial and material resources and people necessary to achieve your visionary strategy?

- How can you acquire the necessary resources without compromising the vision?

Fuel for Thought

In this chapter, you've read a number of questions that can lead you to a business plan that takes you from lofty ideas right on down to action plans. Be aware, though, that these are *just* techniques; simply going through the motions won't guarantee that your vision gets converted to action. The process of creating and harnessing your vision may yield some interesting insights about yourself and your company. Before the information can be transformed into a vibrant, driving corporate vision, it must be energized. Nothing short of the *passion* displayed by leadership will bring about the conversion of vision into reality. Leaders must believe that the world will be a better place for our fellowman if the vision is realized. This belief, of course, must come from within.

But once you let that passion and belief guide you, you will become, as Bob Denckhoff so aptly put it, "possessed," "humbled" and "empowered."

*   *   *

HANDS ON

Mission Possible

Many of the world's greatest thinkers have independently arrived at the conclusion that any idea of merit can be reduced to a single sentence. The same holds for a company mission statement. But sometimes it's hard to find that perfect combination of words that "says it all." The following little game can help.

First, write down the five to seven aspects of your company that you believe capture the essence of your business. Where are the statements similar? Where do they conceptually overlap? Do any of them really say the same thing in different ways (i.e., are seemingly disparate aspects of your company striving for the same goals)? Try combining one or two "overlapping" statements into a short, compact "hybrid" version. Now add a third. Continue until you have one very strong statement that encompasses the TOTALITY of your company.

THE
FOCUSED LENS

Without vision the people perish.
— King Solomon

Living the Corporate Vision

When Jim Balkcom first arrived at Techsonic, the company was located in a 6,000-square-foot metal building on an unfinished site in Eufaula, Alabama. Nevertheless the company's twenty employees were excited and energized by Techsonic's founder, Yank Dean, who had a dream of making high quality depth sounding equipment for bass fishermen. As Balkcom recalls, "I knew this company had tremendous potential. It was a vehicle for accomplishing great things."

And right he was. Today, my friend Jim Balkcom is chairman of Techsonic (known as "Humminbird, USA" to most), having taken over following the unexpected death of its founder. The company now occupies 168,000 square feet, and its 391 employees generate more than $70 million in sales from a broad line of sports fishing depth sounders. The company has gone from what Balkcom describes as a "no name" entity in 1976 to the leader with a 39-percent market share under the "Humminbird" brand name with a 91-percent consumer recognition rating.

Far more than just another financially successful company, though, Techsonic has made an outstanding contribution to the local economy. In 1983, when Balkcom and his senior managers bought the company through a leveraged buyout from the original investor group, they put $700,000 in an employee stock ownership plan. When they cashed out the ESOP in 1987, the fund had grown to $7 million.

"The people who believed in our vision were the winners," he notes with pride. "Some of them hadn't even graduated from high school and lived in economically depressed rural Alabama. Now they have $50,000, $60,000, $100,000 in their retirement plans. There were tears of joy in people's eyes when we announced the figures."

Not surprisingly, what initially attracted Balkcom to Techsonic keeps him there. "I first saw an organization that allowed people to develop what God had given them to the highest potential," he says. "I saw a company that understood the dignity of all people. I saw a unique opportunity to grow with a company that provided outstanding customer service. That's what Techsonic is all about today."

Customers and suppliers immediately appreciate the people-orientation at Techsonic. "Sales reps fight to get the Eufaula territory just to come down here — even ones from New York," Balkcom says with a chuckle. "That's because it doesn't matter what you're selling. We treat our vendors like we treat our associates and customers."

But how has Balkcom managed to infuse nearly 400 people with his vision? "When you have twenty people and a couple of senior managers, communicating the vision is easy," he admits. "You just talk to people every day. All the time. They'll understand your vision and feeling. They see you react on a day-to-day basis, so they see you living your words.

"As we grew, we had to devise other techniques," Balkcom continues. "About seven years ago, our volume was about $11 million. We knew that as we grew to $50 million, we had to start etching out beliefs and values in stone if we were going to maintain a vision based on the dignity of people. Otherwise, things would just get too big and our ideals might get lost. So my partners and I sat down and wrote out our corporate values. Then, over the next six to eight months, we worked with all our associates and honed down the values."

Balkcom's honing resulted in this list:

CUSTOMER SERVICE – Our most important responsibility.

SUPERIOR QUALITY – In each product and service.

PROFESSIONALISM – Striving to use our abilities to do the best possible.

PERSONAL AND CAREER GROWTH – A unique opportunity for each associate.

REWARD FOR INDIVIDUAL PERFORMANCE – Financial reward for outstanding performance in achieving corporate goals.

ENVIRONMENT – Safe, clean, challenging and fun.

PHYSICAL FITNESS – Necessary for productive and creative minds.

LONG-TERM PROFITABILITY – A measure of success necessary to provide all others and increase the value of our ESOP.

As Balkcom proudly explains, these values aren't just part of a "to do" list that people tuck in their drawer. Rather, they're principles to live by. To help keep them on people's minds, Balkcom had them printed on laminated wallet-sized cards. Some associates have carried their cards in their pockets for the past eight years.

To reinforce the importance of the corporate value cards, Techsonic defies conventional wisdom once a month and shuts down the plant for an hour and a half, shifting its phone system to an answering service. During this meeting, which Balkcom describes as "a time for caring and sharing," various awards are given out and problems are aired. As part of every meeting, everyone's name is placed in a hat. If the person who is chosen from the hat can recite the corporate values, he gets a $50 bill on the spot. The meeting always ends in prayer, asking that any success enjoyed by the company be used to the glory of God.

Also, during his random walks through a department, Balkcom is known for stopping an associate and saying, with a grin, "Pull out your corporate value card!" If the associate has his or her card, everyone in the department gets a $5 bill. If not, no one in the department gets a reward.

Far more than just a means of generating some extra pocket money and stimulating positive peer pressure, the words on the cards have become key operating principles for everyone in the company.

"Associates actually use them to help make important decisions," Balkcom explains. "For example, while considering an acquisition, our controller and I toured the plant. The controller took out his corporate value card, studied it for a moment, then turned to me and said, 'Jim, I don't think we can make this environment safe, clean, challenging and fun.' So we decided not to buy the company. That gave me a great deal of satisfaction. I knew we were really living the corporate values when we could pass up a good opportunity because it conflicted with our vision."

Living the corporate values also manifests in people's

daily lives. Says Balkcom, "The corporate values don't end at five o'clock. Associates think about the values at home, while they're on vacation . . . anywhere. One of our associates walked into a K-Mart and was shocked at the Techsonic display. The products were scratched, dusty and poorly arranged. She talked to the manager who said he'd be glad to improve it if she provided new display goods. So she came to us and we empowered her to take action by giving her the resources she needed to make a *great* display. That's just one little example of how people live out the corporate values outside of work."

Perhaps nothing bespeaks Techsonic's first corporate value—customer service—better than the business cards that everyone receives after they've been working at the company for two years. All associates get a box of cards, whether they're in management or maintenance. And they all have the same title: "Customer Service." Even the chairman's card reads, Jim Balkcom, Customer Service. "This really commits everyone to the cause," Balkcom notes. "And it especially shows at the monthly associate meetings when I ask, 'Whose primary responsibility is customer service?' You know what happens? Three hundred ninety-one hands go straight up in the air!"

*   *   *

People Power

As Jim Balkcom proves, when leaders of a company are committed to a clear-sighted, boundless vision, everyone else follows suit, leading to a state of "applied vision." In fact, by focusing the visionary lens so that the light shines throughout the entire company, you create an environment in which people are empowered to take chances, test ideas and make mistakes. Yes, make mistakes. In a traditional corporate setting, "mistake" is often synonymous with "end of the career rope," so people are leery of the unknown or the unproven.

But as any successful entrepreneur will tell you, risks and rewards are directly proportional, and the only way to maximize your investment of brainpower, time and money and the only way to create a state of "continuous improvement" in an organization is to continually take carefully calculated risks.

Beyond the tangible rewards of probing the unknown, empowering people with your organization's vision has a practical benefit. If people know what's expected of them, you don't have to waste time teaching them what to do. Be a paragon of ethical behavior, and you don't have to explain the importance of acting in a right manner with customers, suppliers and fellow employees. Show that you care about every customer and every employee as if they were the most important people in the world, and your associates will do likewise. Ignite a spark, and you'll fire up the engines of change.

Just how do you focus the lens and harness the driving energy that comes from a clear organizational vision? First you must have a visionary idea which becomes your mission or reason to exist as an organization. Then your strategy and set of working tactics become ways to communicate and implement a clear-sighted vision through the entire structure of your company or organization. This chapter describes a number of techniques that you can use to create the communication links that tie everyone in the company together, from the executive suite to the assembly line and back again.

The Benefits of Sharing Your Vision

First and foremost, no vision can bear fruit if it doesn't have the support of people throughout the organization. You can have the purest desires to serve your fellowman, but if the company lacks quality products and caring people, your efforts will be continually frustrated.

Employees are guided and energized either by a united, clearly understood vision or by their personal impression of the big picture. A vision that is effectively communicated throughout the entire company is vital to pull energies together and focus them on specific objectives. Your organization takes on a new energy.

In addition to enjoying this primary benefit, if you run "by the vision" as well as "by the numbers," you'll experience the following types of positive results:

- You'll attract quality people who seek more than employment for pay; you'll attract people who seek higher goals and tend to stay with the job for longer stints than in conventional settings.

- Your people will be self-energized and will work until the day's tasks are done. Done, that is, from *their* perspective, which often means working well beyond normal business hours.

- People in your company will focus on serving the customer rather than carving up in-house territory for building personal empires.

- Your people won't be afraid to try something new because they see the customer as the ultimate arbiter of right and wrong.

- You will continually hear of "positive surprises" which result from people doing unexpected things that add value to the product or service or enhance the company in some important way.

- People will seek responsibility and growth opportunities well beyond their current level of competence. As they grow, the company grows, too.

- A sense of excitement and pride will pervade the company.

- Positive peer pressure will be exerted to meet the customer's needs in the most effective manner. Efficiency and customer satisfaction result.

- People will adopt a sense of ownership in the company; they will speak with pride of having helped build *our* company.

- Lasting friendships, deep respect and trust will develop among those who "buy in" to the vision. Those who don't "buy in" tend to seek employment elsewhere—either on their own or with some encouragement from others on the team.

A Tale of Two Companies

Two case studies illustrate the key role of shared vision in the success of a company.

The first entails an automotive parts company, Mr. Gasket. In the early 1960s, the company's founder, stock car racing enthusiast Joseph Hrudka, sought a better type of engine gasket that wouldn't melt down under high heat. He found the answer in a space-age material supplied by NASA. First, he gave away the new gaskets to his friends, then he began selling them for a dollar. Eventually, he set up shop in his mother's basement, hoping to make $10,000 a year. Beyond his wildest expectations, he grossed $600,000 in the first two years, and a public offering later brought in $1.8 million. Ten years later he sold the company to W. R. Grace for a tidy $17 million.

This could have been the end of a classic rags-to-riches story, but the saga continued as Grace managed to drive its new acquisition deep into the ground. Gone from Mr. Gasket were all the racing aficionados who hung out at the track and lived to help racers achieve better performance. Instead, pinstriped MBA-types reduced the product line to a set of catalog items on a computer printout. Decisions that Hrudka and his crew could make over coffee and donuts in ten minutes took months of slogging through committee meetings and a bureaucratic morass.

Over the next ten years, the company oozed so much red ink that Grace finally cajoled Hrudka into coming out of retirement (he'd taken up antique car and Victorian home renovation), selling him back his original company for $4 million. Hrudka practically revitalized the company overnight, sending the management professionals packing and bringing back the dedicated people who helped build his company in the first place. Within five years the company not only stabilized, but its people introduced scores of new automotive parts that generate a handsome $150 million in sales today.

The second case study involves my own company, Oster Communications. In 1981, Oster Communications acquired Commodity Communications Corporation, which provided real-time futures price quotes to hedgers and traders. At first, Oster Communications tried a "hands off" policy of letting the new company run its own show. The reins of the acquired company were turned over to a manager who had a background in a large corporation and a corporate "control" mentality; he had controls in place to monitor activities, order flow and cash flow. He also had the "right boxes" in his organizational chart, and no one was allowed out of the box to which he or she was assigned. Job descriptions were clearly defined. Heaven forbid you should stick your nose in someone else's business!

Under this manager's rule, few important papers were signed by department heads; everything had to cross his desk. Managers had to wait in line for decisions. Important opportunities were missed.

Moreover, within weeks, a wall went up between the home office and the acquired company. Joint projects were stymied as people pointed the finger and assigned blame rather than working out problems. Attempts to explain how their combined resources could lead to the realization of Oster Communications' vision fell on deaf ears. Over the course of the next two years, the earnings from the acquired company steadily declined as the customer base contracted by 50 percent.

Regretfully, the course of the company was only reversed after several presidents failed at the task. We went through almost 100-percent turnover of people during a five-year period. Those who were used to an "organization chart mentality" were threatened by a more creative approach and sought employment elsewhere.

Finally, a new president, Rex Wilmore, an associate of mine for nearly twenty years, was promoted from within. He carried the corporate vision to the subsidiary. He redefined the vision and the product line with the participation of front-line staff and intense interaction with customers, listening to their needs. The result? A new and innovative product line, driven by the sense of pride and ownership by people in the subsidiary company. And a nice niche in a profitable global market for financial futures news and price analysis.

The company phased out its old product line and offered a new real-time futures price quote, news and analysis service that became the talk of the industry. The company grew and developed a reputation of caring for customers and serving them as family under the new leadership. This represents a complete turnaround in corporate culture and reputation in a matter of months.

Positive Results From a Positive Environment

Just as it's critical for a leader to do away with negative influences during the vision birthing process, it's important to have an environment that enables and encourages people throughout the company to think positively. People generally want to be builders, to be in on "the ground floor," to be part of the founding team. But if they're going to leave the safety of their job description and commit a major part of their life to building your vision, to a new product or to a new service, they must be able to do so without doubts.

This requires creating a positive corporate culture in which the entrepreneurial spirit is unleashed in every business associate. There's no room for negative people in this environment. One bad apple can neutralize the enthusiasm of a half-dozen positive, highly motivated people.

Fortunately, though, once optimism and enthusiasm are on a roll, negative people find they just do not harmonize with the new corporate culture, so they either change their tune or find an excuse to quit or get fired. You can accelerate the process by trying to identify people who may be disruptive and giving them the choice of working for another company where they may be more comfortable.

A positive environment also means an atmosphere in which people can think independently and speak their minds without worrying about being criticized or punished. Often this can be facilitated by taking key people "off site," as Bob Denckhoff did when he formulated his new vision for Missouri Encom (see chapter 3). In a totally new environment, whether it's a hotel seminar room, the meeting house of a retreat or some other outside setting, people are likely to loosen up. Encourage them to speak from the hearts and minds, because *anything* goes.

The best way to get the ball rolling is to bare your own soul, telling people your hopes for them and the company. This works whether you're dealing with a ten-person outfit or a company with 10,000 employees. Don Williams, managing partner of Trammel Crow (which happens to have 10,000 employees), says, "One of my roles is to repeat the company vision in messages I deliver at company meetings. We have a written philosophy and code of ethics, but our leaders must continually repeat our vision of being a good, profitable and enduring real estate development company."

You can go even further and *tell* people that you expect them to become integral, participating members of your team. At first, people may react with suspicion, especially if their previous work environments have been built around highly structured pecking orders and chains of command. Be patient and help draw people out by asking them to tell you how their jobs can contribute to your overall goal. Explain how they too will benefit materially and spiritually by striving to apply the vision.

When your initial off-site session is completed (you'll probably want to repeat it at least once a year), your team leaders should leave with a clear mandate for helping others in the organization to understand and embrace the vision. That's the real payoff from the session: You multiply your effort and leverage your energy through the critical mass of positive thinkers. If ten people participated in the session and each one passes the driving energy on to five other people, then fifty people in your company will be tuned in to the vision. If each of those fifty people go out and pass the vision along to five more people, then 250 more people will join the movement.

In this way, a single effort can leverage itself across a company of hundreds, even thousands, of people. Once a group of thinkers achieves a critical mass and begins to generate its own enthusiasm through a shared set of objectives and values, good things begin to happen.

Vision Training

In addition to the "top down" approach of energizing key people and then turning them loose to energize others, companies can engage in "vision training." Vision training should be part of the other types of education that take place during the normal course of business. Below I've described some opportunities to incorporate vision training into your various employee education programs.

Orientation Sessions for New Employees

The leaders of a company have an outstanding opportunity to present the view from the top to new associates during orientation sessions. At this time, the vision should be cast in terms that will personally affect everyone in the room. For example, "If the customer is happy, he'll buy our product. We have a chance of making a profit and providing challenging careers only when we have a growing customer base." This establishes a direct cause and effect relation in the mind of the new associates, linking their personal success with customer satisfaction.

Karl Albrecht, author of *At America's Service*, states:

> The employee orientation process is frequently a huge missed opportunity in many organizations. Consider the significance of a new employee's entry into the organizational culture the first day, the first week, the first month of employment. During this critical period the new person reads the corporate environment, sees what other people do, hears how they talk, finds out what they think, and begins to form the basis of his or her own work attitudes and habits that will probably continue for a long time. Why leave this critical process of perception and attitude formation to chance?

Product Training

Employees who know the nitty gritty of your product

line will be more responsive to customers. They can interpret customer complaints more effectively and make meaningful suggestions. In a sense, then, routine product training and vision training can become one and the same. Product managers can role play in scenarios that portray the buying process. This kind of training clarifies everyone's vision of how they fit and how specific products fit into the larger corporate mission.

Customer Training

At Oster Communications, business associates are encouraged to go to company-sponsored seminars where customers are learning about the product. In this atmosphere, associates learn to think in terms of customer benefits as they overhear customers respond to specific features and benefits of each product.

Your company, too, can prosper by putting as many employees as possible in meetings with customers, especially those whose job descriptions would normally dictate that they never even *see* a customer. At such meetings, employees will hear how the company's products help customers achieve their objectives, and they will become more deeply committed to customer service. This in turn will lead to improvement in the product line. A company's employees are much more effective when they understand the mindset of the customer and how the company's product or service can help the customer achieve his objectives.

Skills Training

Hands-on classes that teach specific skills, such as computer usage, word processing, etc., can show a person how to perform a specific function beyond the current demands of his or her job. Such training makes employees more versatile and enables them to take a more active role in the fulfillment of the vision. For this reason, it's important to use skills training sessions as opportunities to reinforce the purpose for the company's existence and its long-term goals.

Industry Training

If a person is going to grow in your business or organization, he or she must have a good understanding about the players in your industry and their needs, general industry trends and cutting-edge issues. Some of this information can be picked up through trade magazines, but a sense of the real world can come only from hands-on experience. Some types of training that bring new associates in contact with actual customers are, therefore, excellent means for promoting an appreciation of the customer's needs and the company's vision for fulfilling them. Vision training and industry training go hand in hand.

Attitude Training

The best attitude training is done in-house by peers who have embraced the company vision and can excite others about it. Frequent half-day and full-day review and planning sessions also provide an opportunity for associates to talk about their successes and their challenges. Brainstorming sessions on current problems and opportunities cause many to share the vision of creating the future. Those meetings also give employees a chance to socialize with other people in the company, so their knowledge of your organization and appreciation of its vision will be constantly reinforced.

Miscellaneous Opportunities: Daily Reminders

In addition to the above training opportunities, there are numerous little opportunities for reinforcing the application of the vision on a day-to-day basis. Memos, company newsletters, employee handbooks and other documents and publications can help remind people why the company exists and the important role they play in translating your visionary goals into reality.

Time management, goal formation and strategic objective forms can also be of help in getting people to articulate their sense of the vision and how they fit into it. In the Appendix you'll find a number of self-explanatory forms for helping people organize their objectives and keep their actions aligned with the leader's boundless vision. At Oster Communications, every associate uses these and other forms to develop short-term and long-term strategies. The forms, which give people a chance to reflect on their professional, personal and spiritual goals, serve as a means by which team leaders and mentors can help their advisees develop realistic approaches for accomplishing their objectives within the desired time frame.

Hiring: Front-Line Opportunity for Communicating the Vision

Nothing affords you a better chance to enlighten people about your company's vision than the hiring process. During the interview process, you can help people understand what they're buying into — that they're not just signing up for a nine-to-five job. Recall Bob Denckhoff's concept of "ruthless hiring" as a means of ensuring the integrity of the vision. Every time you bring someone new into the company, you're in effect adding a person who can carry and help focus the vision. The hiring process should be one of education, enlightenment and soul searching.

I like to explain our vision, our progress and our plans to a prospective employee in enthusiastic tones, then watch his or her eyes. I can tell in a minute if this is a vision he or she understands and gets excited about. If the next ten minutes of conversation centers around fulfilling that vision, it is a positive clue that I'm talking to a "live candidate."

The more people know about your organization before they sign on, the less you'll have to weed out those who are seeking only their own advancement and a quick buck. You will tend to attract the kind of quality, caring people that you want in your organization if they are tuned in and turned on by your vision.

*　*　*

HANDS ON

Vision Check

Caution! The following little game will most likely yield some unexpected results, so be prepared for some potentially unsettling news. More important, be prepared to develop the right tactics you need to bring about change.

Take the mission statement you wrote in chapter 3 and randomly select a diverse group of associates from within your organization. Make sure the group includes the following kinds of people:

- top managers

- middle managers

- sales people

- assistants and secretaries

- receptionists

- production people

- the delivery people

- maintenance people

Ask them to write a paragraph about *their* perceptions of the company's vision. It's best if you prompt them with specific questions, rather than asking them to free associate on paper.

Next, go outside the company and assemble another group of observers, including:

- customers

- suppliers

- family

- friends

Give them the vision test, also prompting them for answers.

Now compare everyone's description of the vision to your own. How well does it correspond? In what areas are people out of sync with each other and with you? And what can you do about harmonizing their views with your own?

THE THINKING
WORKER

*You are a manipulator when you try to persuade
people to do something that is not in their best interests but is in yours. You are a motivator when
you find goals that will be good for both sides,
then weld together a high-achieving, high-morale
partnership to achieve them.*

—Alan Loy McGinnes, **Bringing Out the Best in People**

Motivating Those Associated With the Vision

"The old approach to getting employees to do what you
wanted was called intimidation," comments motivational
expert and author Lewis Timberlake. "That period was
followed by manipulation—the old carrot-and-stick approach where management promised things that it might
or might not actually deliver. Next, we had the 'cheerleader
approach'—clap your hands, jump around. Today, we have
what I call 'internal motivation'—see what a person can do
when he or she gets internally turned on."

Timberlake has seen all forms of motivation in his
years of consulting with clients such as Pfizer, IBM, GTE
and other major corporations, and even some smaller ones
like our own Oster Communications. Lew has had a

profound impact on my own thinking on how to encourage people to grow. Lew believes that internal goal setting is the most promising and productive because it is mutually beneficial to both the company and the people who work for it.

Internal goal setting is really a process, according to Timberlake. "First, address one of the most fundamental of human needs: to be loved. To get someone fired up, you have to show him that you really *do* care about helping him achieve his goals. Then you've got to prove that his goals can be fulfilled by doing his job as well as possible."

To show that you care about an employee, Timberlake suggests, find out what he or she really wants. "A computer programmer's needs will be different from a salesperson's or assembly worker's needs. One size doesn't fit all."

Maybe the computer operator is looking for educational opportunities so he can get a management position. Perhaps the salesperson is seeking a better territory. And the fellow on the assembly line might really want to save up and buy a new pickup truck. In Timberlake's view, you must show each of these people how, through superb performance and an eye to customer satisfaction, they can get what they want. In other words, "You have to overlay their goals onto the company's goals."

"You can't be idealistic and assume that all people will necessarily want to lay themselves out for the customer," Timberlake warns. "Sometimes they first have to believe they're making progress in finding themselves. For some people, the security of knowing who they are may come early in life; for others, it may never come and you'll always have to focus on how the job at hand benefits their particular needs."

The final stage in the goal setting process is to be a truly selfless servant. Says Timberlake, "This can come about only when people operate from a strong basis of security. If you don't love yourself, you can't love another. Christ was so successful because He came in totally satisfied with Himself; He knew that He was put on earth to fulfill a great mission. This basis of self-love and understanding is the real meaning of the servant's attitude."

Even if only a handful of your employees are secure enough to adopt the servant's attitude in their daily work, Timberlake encourages company leaders to be patient. "Life is a series of goal-settings," he says joyously. "Each time you get to a goal, you reach for the next. You have to believe that down deep, everyone is potentially able to reach the point where they can know and love themselves and their fellowman. This ladder of continual growth and personal evolution—I think it's what we're here for."

*   *   *

Beyond Manipulation

For people who have trained at large organizations, the concept of motivation and manipulation are often synonymous. Managers frequently attend seminars that allegedly teach them how to be more sensitive when, in fact, they often walk out with a bag of tricks for duping people into doing more work for less pay. In this view, the term "human resources" takes on new meaning; it becomes a euphemism for "disposable people."

Nothing can be more self-defeating than to treat employees as raw material in a mill: consumed at one end and spit out at the other. Employees—your "associates," really—are the key to your company's success and survival, whether you're Digital Electronic Corporation with 115,000 people on the payroll or the Mom-and-Pop corner store with one part-time helper.

This chapter explores various techniques for helping your associates achieve a higher level of understanding themselves and takes them a step closer to adopting the selfless style of the servant. It also explores the basic tools for translating the leader's clear-sighted vision into the day-to-day work of each individual in the company. Such "applied vision" can come about only in a setting that allows people to reach their full potential in terms of their personal, spiritual and professional goals. This setting is best described as an "opportunity climate."

Creating an Opportunity Climate

If you follow Lewis Timberlake's line of thinking, the best way to help people set and achieve their internal goals is to create an environment in which they can rise to the opportunities set before them. An "opportunity climate" is based on the belief that we have God-given potential for growth and creativity.

By starting with this fundamental faith in the God-created uniqueness of each human being, you tap the special potential of each and every associate in your company rather than setting each one in some predetermined mold. And by tapping unique individual abilities, you fulfill each person's needs for personal success while strengthening your company's ability to grow and prosper.

The opportunity climate is one in which every associate feels a responsibility to grow on the job to new levels of understanding and skill and higher levels of responsibility.

Anatomy of an Opportunity Climate

An opportunity climate is an environment in which hierarchy and rigid rules are replaced by team spirit and flexibility. It is an environment that allows people to treat failure as a teacher and to test new ideas without fear of retribution. Most important, it is an environment that treats people as the company's main asset and does everything possible to see that people flourish and reach their maximum potential.

Contrast the opportunity climate approach with the organizational chart mentality, sometimes called the "Harvard Business School" model, which views the corporation basically as an economic entity. In this approach, the organization is built to serve the needs of efficient deployment of capital and labor; in other words, to earn a profit.

According to this philosophy, you first define the product, then you define the organization needed to support it. Next, you plan strategies and objectives, and define the various organizational functions. The organization is then subdivided into its basic components, divisions are broken down into departments, departments into branches, branches into sections and, finally, sections into individual work units.

At the individual work unit level, you define individual jobs, one per person. For each job, there's a description and a tightly defined set of standards and measures developed by efficiency experts. Once all this is done, you hire workers, then plug them into the job slots.

In his bestselling book, *At America's Service,* Karl Albrecht notes: "The Harvard model is essentially an inhuman model; i.e., the focus of thought is on structure rather than people. The language of a business school is one of organization theory, finance and accounting, strategy, marketing methods, policy, common management systems and an occasional course in personnel."

In the final analysis, Albrecht continues, the Harvard model is all about profit: "At the bottom line, the balance sheet and income statement become prayer books and hymnals in the worship of profit." He points out that "in reality the *people* are the capital, labor and the product all rolled into one. They are an asset that appreciates in value, and this is the concept no accounting model has yet managed to incorporate."

Companies that go beyond the accounting model and create high opportunity climates know the truth in Albrecht's words. As a result, they realize the enormous benefits that come about when people are allowed to grow and thrive. Some of the major benefits of the opportunity "model" are described below.

What Happens When You Create an Opportunity Climate?

In an opportunity or growth climate, no one wastes time on turf battles, because there is no turf to speak of. That is, there are no corporate ladders to climb. Salespeople and other associates can earn more than their immediate supervisors or team leader, so there is no economic incentive to become a manager, vice president or some other figurehead on the totem pole. People see winning customer loyalty as their challenge, not winning a battle for recognition with their counterpart down the hall by gaining a new level on the organizational chart.

This dissolution of hierarchy is a positive trend seen in more and more growth companies. It can even work on a large scale. The W. L. Gore Company, for example, is based on what is known as a "lattice structure" which, at first blush, looks more like a tribal initiation rite than a business. At Gore, there are no real job descriptions; new associates float about until they find a niche that works for them. They also must find a "mentor" who will take them under his/her wing and coach them until they're ready to fly on their own, at which point they can begin mentoring a new associate of their own.

Another noted absence of hierarchy can be found at

the Honda plant in Marysville, Ohio. While job descriptions do exist at the facility, there is little jockeying for position. Everyone, including the general manager, wears a white jump suit with his or her name stitched on top. This "dress code" symbolically levels the playing field and puts everyone on an equal footing.

In addition to the dissolution of hierarchies that hamper productivity, opportunity climates offer a number of impressive benefits to the company and its associates:

They encourage creativity through frequent brainstorming sessions. The brainstorming yields new ideas that enable the company to better serve its customers. During brainstorming sessions, people are not afraid to speak their minds, so every new idea is taken seriously. New projects are given fair tests and, if the test flops, the associates move on to something else.

Opportunity climates enable people to select their co-workers. In an opportunity climate, hiring is usually not complete until the applicant has been interviewed by other associates who will be working closely side-by-side. This is particularly important in situations where one person's failure to come through can affect the performance of the whole team. To give 110 percent, people need to be comfortable with their fellow associates and have the confidence of knowing that they'll do their job.

Opportunity climates engender mutual respect. Since associates are involved in the process of determining who will be working with them, they become invested in their co-workers' talent bank. This allows them to mutually encourage each other and engage in open discussions where strengths and weaknesses can be discussed in non-threatening ways. Poor performers will be encouraged by team members who cheer them on to the finish line. This can make the difference between someone who ultimately makes the team and someone who has to seek employment at another organization.

They foster high performance standards. By attracting people whose professional skills are worthy of respect, the culture generates unwritten performance standards for the quality and quantity of work. People, especially younger associates, learn these standards by observing others and, therefore, know what is expected of them. This frees up managers to focus on more important things than policing the time clock or the out-baskets. Instead, they are finding new and creative ways to satisfy customers and boost the profitability of the company.

They support the spirit of independence. In an opportunity climate, most associates are free to carry out their mission in their own unique way. While everyone knows the job they must complete, and the standards to which they must adhere, there are always infinite ways to execute the tasks at hand. These variations on a theme often yield rich and surprising alternatives that improve the efficiency of the process and the quality of the end product or service.

Opportunity climates encourage people to compare self with self, not self with others. When people compare themselves to where they were a year ago, rather than against the progress of a fellow associate, they set new and realistic standards. This enables people to advance their abilities in the absence of a stressful and competitive environment.

They enable people to feel trusted and invested with authority. The need to be trusted, like the need to be loved, is basic. In the workday world, the need to be granted increasing amounts of authority is also fundamental. The manager who must approve every new thing that everyone does in his department is a serious stumbling block to personal and, therefore, corporate growth.

They provide the basis for tailored training programs.

Some skills can be taught through training programs, while others can only be learned by allowing a person to make increasingly significant judgments while working with a mentor (see below). Further, there are some functions where the only training is "baptism by fire." All three educational functions can operate equally well in an opportunity climate, giving leaders the chance to custom tailor the kind of training and help programs they need to bring people up to speed in their work.

Opportunity climates make it easy for "mentoring" to occur. Mentoring is the process by which a person with a senior level of experience takes a personal interest in someone at a junior level. The mentor is not only interested in the junior person's professional life, but in his or her personal life as well. In this way, a mentor is looked up to as a mother or father figure with a high level of experience, knowledge and wisdom, and the junior person feels it's an honor to be in the mentor's presence.

The mentor understands the junior associate's needs within the company, and helps him or her to figure out what to do next, what skills to hone, etc. This advisory action is more than a kind-hearted gesture and an effective means of training; it is a special opportunity for veterans of the company to translate the leader's ideals into practice.

Finally, and perhaps most significant, is the fact that *opportunity climates are conducive to a sense of teamwork.* These days, more and more companies are beginning to realize that teamwork is a key to success. In the high-tech arena, a number of companies are adopting what is known in Silicon Valley as "smart teams." These teams include a cross section of departmental heads who join forces to make decisions and solve problems, rather than operating as autonomous fiefdoms.

Xerox, after taking a drubbing from Japanese competitors in the small copier market, now links purchasing people with engineers and others involved in the R&D process; when an engineer wants to use a certain type of plastic in a new part, it's a team effort that investigates the cost effectiveness of taking that approach. This saves the company from potentially expensive mistakes and brings together people who normally might never see each other even though they play pivotal roles in providing top-notch customer service.

Tips for Creating an Opportunity Climate

1. Really care about the people around you. You can't fake a caring and open environment. Prove the depth of your vision by becoming more visible and available to your associates. Drop in on people. When they come to see you, put your feet up on your desk and talk to them in a person-to-person way that breaks down the "boss/employee" barrier. That barrier is a major impediment to creativity.

2. Tell people directly and openly about your hopes and plans for the future and how they can help turn that dream into reality.

3. Ask people about their objectives and explore ways that they can mesh with yours.

4. Give people positive strokes, lots of verbal pats on the back. Stop off at people's desks and say to people, "Hey, I really like the way you did this. Keep it up!"

5. Be consistent in the way you pass out rewards.

6. Bring out the best in people by sponsoring contests for thinking up the best ideas. Be there personally to hand out the prizes or commendations. Show that you're proud of people.

7. Maintain an open door policy. De-emphasize the corporate structure and focus on creativity. The pecking

order threatens a lot of people and prevents them from getting involved in brainstorming. At the same time, don't take away all familiar signposts overnight; you can literally scare an organization into non-performance if you give people too much freedom when they aren't used to it. Gradually offer the people the autonomy they need to think in high gear.

Building a Winning Team

To understand what pulls a team together, start with the opposite of a team: the organizational chart which isolates each individual. People who operate with the organizational chart mentality frequently believe in the philosophy of "a day's work for a day's pay," forty hours a week, fifty-two weeks a year (less vacation), and so on. Further, when people believe that their only responsibility is to take care of a certain job function, they develop an apathetic attitude toward customers and the people in the organization who contact customers.

Worst of all, when people are taught to live exclusively by rules, the rules become more important than customer satisfaction. People are taught to follow the rules and do everything possible to eliminate all traces of human thought and judgment. The result is that no one is authorized to think, so the customer gets the short end of the stick.

The team model allows people to define the size and location of the "organizational chart box." The goal is people oriented, and the result is profit *if* and when people-needs are met. The team model eliminates the traditional pecking order by refocusing people's attention on a shared goal and the spirit of cooperation, rather than "Who's ahead of me and how do I get beyond him?" The result is that more things get done with higher quality and less effort.

Energizing a Team

A clear-sighted vision should be the seed for a team. As the vision spreads throughout the company, it creates a powerful spirit of camaraderie and cooperative effort. Be aware, though, that the energy required to build a successful team is inversely proportional to the credibility of the shared vision; the more believable the vision, the less energy it will take to get everyone on board. Credibility is largely established by the leader's enthusiasm, provided that the enthusiasm is genuine. People are not fooled by transparent slogans and, if anything, will respond negatively to them.

Enthusiasm by itself, though, isn't the answer. Taken out of context, it's merely a form of what Lewis Timberlake calls "cheerleading." Members of the team must themselves be enthusiastic so that the positive energy of one person ignites a spark in another, until the process feeds on itself.

Pep talks and motivational speeches are terrific, but the greatest incentives for a team to perform come from direct feedback from the marketplace. When the vision of the company turns into a product or service that helps a customer solve a problem, the team really hits paydirt. No motivational speech can fire up a team more than success in the marketplace properly communicated to each person in the organization.

Realistically, though, can you maintain a team spirit when a company undergoes a period of rapid growth? The answer is "yes," provided that you keep your eyes open. Oster Communications provides a good case study on how growth affects team spirit. Oster Communications was one big team until it had about fifteen or twenty people, at which point it began to develop departmental teams with very little coordination among team leaders. By the time the company hit forty people, walls began to rise between departments and communication barriers began to slow down the flow of information. As time went on, it became more and more difficult for newcomers to catch the vision.

The problem was solved when our associates alerted us to serious communication problems. And we were Oster Communications, where good communication is what we know best. That was a humbling revelation from the grass roots. Now we "dust off" the vision every few months, carry on more brainstorming sessions and customer focus interviews, and form cross-departmental teams which break down communication barriers.

On a larger scale, look at Jim Balkcom's company, Techsonic (see chapter 4). Even with 400 employees, Balkcom still manages to shut down the operation once a month for an hour of caring, sharing and communicating. The result? A company that keeps attracting dedicated people and customers and has attained national prominence.

Tips for Building Strong Teams

1. Make everyone understand that, one way or another, *everyone* plays on a team. People must realize that nothing of significance happens in an organization because of one person; real breakthroughs and ongoing support for novel products and services can come only from a concerted team effort.

2. Do whatever you have to to get everyone on the team involved in brainstorming and problem solving. If you have several verbal people on the team who might naturally dominate a group session, ask the group to write down ideas and decide among themselves which ideas are the best. In this way, everyone gets a chance to be involved in the idea development process.

3. Make some ground rules: No one should be allowed to

say negative things about others in the group during team meetings. Get people to focus on issues, not personalities.

4. Teach the "superstars" not to dominate team meetings with their ideas but to encourage everyone to talk.

5. Form project and problem-solving teams from several departments involved in delivering the organization's product or service. Such teams take a broader look at problems and opportunities and tend to break down "departmental territoriality."

Going One-on-One

Teams are built and strengthened through the continual interaction of people and the open sharing of information. In a growing organization, the most effective communication vehicle is the "one-on-one" private, weekly or bi-weekly meetings between team leader and individual members.

The flow of communication in the one-on-one must be two-way. The leader may start off with something like, "Here's how I think you're doing . . . " The team member might begin with, "Here's how I feel about my job, little gripes I'd like to vent, guidance I need, etc." Whatever the mechanics, the goal is to stimulate meaningful interaction that leads to good growth and performance and a more satisfactory work setting.

The one-on-one meeting can have a tremendous impact on corporate culture. The idea sounds so fundamental that it may appear trite at first. But when put into action, the one-on-one can be a powerful communications tool, even if used on an "irregular" basis. Unexpected travel, special meetings, crises and other situations will necessarily disrupt schedules for one-on-one meetings. Even so, you don't need perfect continuity to make one-on-one's an effective tool in your organization. Even when traveling, a phone call at a regular time can accomplish much of the benefit derived from the one-on-one.

The one-on-one is a liberating, empowering meeting even for the team leader who talks constantly with team members during the day. The tone and purpose of the conversation is different when there is a set time of the week or month just to talk heart-to-heart.

One-on-one sessions offer immediate benefits to team leaders, team members and, hence, the company. Here are some of the benefits our company has identified:

Team Leaders

- Elimination of interruptions
- A window into an associate's priorities
- Translation of departmental objectives into individual tasks
- Definition and clarification of expectations

Team Members

- A "safe" haven where they can discuss issues openly and without fear of being criticized
- An appropriate way to "blow off steam"
- A proving ground for new ideas

The Company

- Improved productivity
- An informed staff
- A reduction in finger-pointing

Tips for Maximizing One-on-Ones

Every individual will ultimately develop his or her own one-on-one style. Nevertheless, if you haven't conducted one-on-ones before, a bit of preparation can help you get the most out of them. Here are some specific suggestions for your first sessions:

1. Announce ahead of time that you'll be doing regular one-on-ones with everyone on your team and that the purpose is to find out, "How can we help each other serve the customer better or faster?"

2. Prepare for the meeting by gathering specific observations or questions.

3. Start the session with some positive observation on some of the things that the team member is doing well.

4. Break the ice by asking questions that require thoughtful answers. For example, "How would you suggest we make improvements in area X, Y or Z?" rather than questions that can be answered with a "yes" or "no."

5. Make sure that the meetings don't degenerate into sessions where data is merely passed along from one person to another. Stay focused on "What do you believe?" "What do you feel?" and "How do you think we can better serve our customers?"

6. Never rush a one-on-one or make the associate feel that he or she is being "squeezed in."

7. Discuss any negatives in terms of a standard, then discuss optional ways to help improve performance in the areas in question.

8. Cover specific items of priority from your schedule just to verify who is doing what and when they are doing it.

9. At the conclusion, summarize the session briefly to review each party's position, listing and clarifying any specifics to be done.

Finally, be aware that sessions will begin with "big picture" issues and eventually shift into specifics like "things I'm doing" and "things you're doing." When this happens, be sure to redirect the thrust back to the big questions, such as "How do you feel about 'X'?" This is essential to maintaining the flow of communication in both directions and building the momentum, commitment and focus that becomes the lifeblood of a growing organization.

Applied Vision

So far, this book has covered the basics of forming a vision and communicating it along with specific priorities through all levels of your organization. If the vision has been well defined, people will have a clear-sighted view of their work and the mission of the company. If the vision is meaningful, people will begin to apply it in all of their actions, and begin to use it as a filter for viewing the world.

All tasks, big or small, will suddenly be reviewed from the perspective of the vision, and people will ask, "Does this further the mission? Will I be helping the customer? Will I be helping my fellow team members?" The next step is to go beyond the traditional walls of the corporation and apply the vision when dealing with the rest of the world—your customers, suppliers and even competitors. These are the topics of the next three chapters.

*   *   *

HANDS ON

1. *Recruit Yourself.* Company leaders often forget the fact that they, too, were employees at some point in their lives. Therefore, it's useful to turn the tables and look at your company from the other side of the coin. Take a sheet of paper and draw a line down the center. On the left side, make a list of the ten most important attributes of a potential employer. On the right side, describe how your company stacks up for each entry. When you finish, ask yourself whether you'd want to be hired by your

company today. If so, how could you make your organization even more desirable? If not, where is the company lacking? Whatever the outcome, develop an action plan for improvement.

2. *Rate Your Opportunity Quotient.* The following self-test will help you assess your company's opportunity level. Take your time, and answer each question as honestly as possible on a scale of 1 (meaning "very little") to 5 ("very much").

1. Job descriptions don't mean a lot in our company—people just know what to do.

2. People in our company are encouraged to innovate.

3. People understand that the only competition is the company across the street—not the office down the hall.

4. Information flows "sideways" as well as top to bottom; decisions are made on the basis of a broad cross section of views.

5. Pressure gets vented in our company before it reaches an explosive level. It's also vented in a positive way that helps people learn and grow.

6. People don't feel managed; rather, they feel inspired and led toward a higher goal.

7. Our culture builds in time for an associate to follow a hunch and doesn't threaten punishment if the idea flops.

8. People in our company look out for new associates and help them learn the ropes.

9. If you suddenly quit or meet with some unexpected tragedy, *anyone* in our company could, with some coaching, become the new leader.

If your score is:

40 - 45	You have an exceptionally high opportunity quotient, and your company should excel.
30 - 39	You have a strong opportunity climate and, with some improvements and adjustments, your organization should become a winner.
20 - 29	Your company could strongly benefit by exploring those areas in which you scored less than "3."
9 - 19	Retake this test six months after completing this book and implementing its key tactics.

LIGHT AT THE END
OF THE TUNNEL

It is not the employer who pays wages — he only handles the money. It is the product that pays wages.

— Henry Ford

Walking Like We Talk . . .

"We started talking about Total Quality in 1983," recalls Steve Uhlmann, president and CEO of the Tech Group — six separate companies involved in plastics manufacturing and plastic packaging. At that time, the Tech Group was invited to a Hewlett-Packard vendor seminar that focused on quality as a means of lowering costs and making continual improvements.

Following the seminar, Frank Mead, general manager, was so excited about the Total Quality concept that he initiated an in-house quality training program at Tech Medical, a division of the company that makes plastic components for the health care industry. "The program consisted of biweekly training programs," Uhlmann explains. "Each one was based on the HP seminar material. Everyone in the division attended for about a year. In the second year, the training was reduced to once a month."

The meetings used a number of classic books, including W. Edwards Deming's *Out of the Crisis*, Schonberger's *World Class Manufacturing*, and Kiyoshi Suzaki's *The New Manufacturing Challenge*. A typical session would cover a chapter from one of the books. Currently, Tech Medical is also using Suzaki's video tapes.

Did it work? "For three years, almost every factor improved," Uhlmann says. "We measure productivity by machine hours per person. Productivity doubled; our sales per employee shot up 70 percent. Inventory turnover was greatly improved. Customer satisfaction was great. And our return rate was one-tenth of the original rate, which was low to begin with—less than 1 percent. Excellent by industry standards!"

At this point, you might imagine that Uhlmann instituted the same quality program at the other five divisions, and that the Tech Group happily profited ever after. Actually, Uhlmann and his associates did try to start a quality program in one other division, bringing in two veterans from Tech Medical.

"Unfortunately, the quality program at Tech Medical began falling apart," Uhlmann admits. "What we found was that we didn't have the depth of training and broad commitment in the Medical group that we thought we had. The Medical division was successful because we had a couple of key people who were maintaining the quality effort."

This taught Uhlmann a vital lesson: Recognize the importance of ongoing outside education, from top management through direct labor. To address that need, Hal Tashman, vice president and partner, struck up an agreement with nearby Gateway Community College in which the Tech Group pays an annual fee to retain a professor strictly for Tech Group employees. Tech employees have 37,000 hours of classroom time available and can sign up for courses ranging from mechanical engineering to pneumatics. "Our goal is to get people to work in a problem-solving environment," says Uhlmann. "We also want to shift people from directed management programs into management facilitation programs."

According to Uhlmann, the biggest problem facing companies that want to start Total Quality programs is getting people to adapt to change: "Managing change is very difficult. The idea of continuous improvement—making gradual improvements in quality—is alien to a lot of people. People are used to having a goal and striving for it. This is different."

How do you change attitudes? "We have a personality profile that identifies different personal styles. It helps people become aware of their own views and to respect the differences of others."

Equally important, Uhlmann stresses that a commitment to continuous improvement has to be 100 percent rooted at the top or else it has no chance of being successful. "Top managers must really be pacesetters. If we think we've arrived and know it all, any attempt for company-wide implementation will be useless. I guess it just comes down to this: We have to walk like we talk."

*   *   *

Revisiting an Old Concept

In one sense, the concept of "quality" is as obvious as can be: Make a good product, offer a good service and customers will beat a path to your door. Why, then, was quality suddenly "discovered" in the late '70s? And why are quality experts suddenly making millions of dollars helping companies make a good product or service? In part, many companies got lazy during the past few decades when resources seemed infinite and American business seemed indomitable. But with the energy crises of the '70s, and the emergence of highly efficient competitors in the Far East, the old ways of thinking about business suddenly became obsolete. To compete in the global marketplace, companies had to think leaner and smarter. And quality has been a key tool in achieving both goals.

Just what exactly, though, does the word *quality* mean? One valid definition is the everyday use of the term: the look and feel and functionality of a product, or the thoroughness of a service.

On another level, Total Quality takes into account the process by which products are made and services are delivered. In the manufacturing sector, Total Quality often takes on a special meaning, where it refers to the process of identifying and eliminating waste. *Waste,* in this context, refers to anything that doesn't add value to the product.

Inefficient systems that duplicate paperwork are wasteful because they cost money but don't add value to anything. Excess raw material or finished goods inventories are similarly wasteful because they tie up valuable cash without contributing anything positive to the product. Defective parts are similarly considered waste because they add no value to a deliverable product. Even a tardy accounts payable department is wasteful in this context; after all, it costs money to have employees spend their time fending off angry vendors, and none of their efforts add value to the product.

This quality way to look at a business can have a dramatic effect on performance. In fact, it's one of the primary reasons that the Japanese have done so well in the automobile industry. Many people assume that Japanese auto makers were able to undercut American companies because they either underpay their workers or use shoddy materials; neither could be further from the truth.

Japanese workers enjoy wage and benefit packages that are the envy of the world. And today, "Made in Japan" means the highest quality components and finished products. (Japanese steel, for example, is some of the finest available.) The real savings come from their relentless pursuit of the elimination of waste.

Among other techniques, the Japanese at Toyota Motors developed the concept of "Just-in-Time," in which materials are delivered many times a day by vendors right to the work stations where they're needed. This eliminates the need to stockpile huge inventories of parts. But this also means that vendors have virtually no margin for error; if they deliver defective materials or parts, the whole show stops. So the onus is on the vendors to do an excellent job of certifying their goods before they're shipped.

With the Toyota system, there is no wasteful "scrap" because vendors are responsible for providing defect-free materials. Paperwork is eliminated because the company shares its parts needs with its vendors, often via computer, so there's no chance of getting bogged down in wasteful layers of purchase orders and requisitions.

These and other aspects of the Just-in-Time system allow the Japanese to produce cars for an average of $1,000 less per auto than their American counterparts. This, of course, translates into a tremendous competitive edge.

The Japanese approach to manufacturing has not gone unnoticed in the United States. Hewlett-Packard, NCR and Xerox have begun focusing on quality and the elimination of waste. Like the Tech Group, they find that their profits dramatically increase through cost control, reduced inventories and other key measures. And since all the processes are geared toward "zero defects," the customer is the ultimate beneficiary of the effort.

The fact is, you don't have to make cars, computers or

copiers to adopt a quality attitude. The concepts of eliminating waste and striving for zero defects can be applied to any business, whether it sells information, widgets or consulting services. Just think of all the duplicate paperwork that exists in a typical company. How much time and energy could people save if most of it could be eliminated?

Think of how "duplicate skills" can be eliminated by the use of personal computers. Traditionally, managers dictated or hand-wrote drafts of letters and memos that would be passed on to a typing pool. Two or more people were therefore necessary to create one printed piece, which is a waste of talent. Today, more and more managers are using PCs to create their own letters, memos and documents, freeing their assistants to learn desktop publishing and other higher level skills.

And think of how much defective material most businesses tolerate. By perpetuating this attitude, they give their employees and vendors a clear message: Waste is business as usual—don't make any attempts to improve. We are tacitly saying that they, too, can produce a certain amount of defective product or render a certain level of unacceptable service. Somehow, sometime, "business as usual" must be redefined by an endless quest for 100-percent quality.

Charting a New Course: Total Quality Control

Can a company really achieve 100-percent defect-free products or services? The answer is less important than whether companies are *willing to strive* for 100 percent, whether their leader's vision encompasses the drive for perfection. When that drive for quality stretches to every operation in the company—i.e., becomes applied vision—it leads to continuous improvement. Continuous improvement means going from 75 percent to 78 percent in a way that doesn't break anyone's back. It means going from 78 percent to 82 percent in the same way. Even if the company achieves a 99.9 percent waste-free, defect-free state, Total Quality Control requires people to keep pushing toward 100 percent.

And when they reach 100 percent? They must continue pushing forward to keep from backsliding. The key point is that under a program of gradual improvement, target figures and dates should still be established, but the focus must be on the improvement *process* itself.

For many managers, this is a novel, even jarring, approach. As Steve Uhlmann pointed out, some managers are thrown by the idea of continuous improvement if they've come from an environment in which top management sets a target figure and everyone scrambles to meet it, realistic or not. The problem with this approach is that such improvement campaigns are generally born from crises, so they're driven by fear rather than positive striving.

Often, too, top managers issue goals that they know are impossible, figuring that if "I want to get 85 percent, I'd better demand 98 percent." Unfortunately, most people catch on quickly to such inflated expectations and accordingly adjust their efforts downward to what they know are realistic performance levels. This not only undermines management's campaign, but it also turns the campaign into a game in which people spend more time uncovering the hidden rules than doing what needs to be done.

With a Total Quality approach, people accept and welcome gradual improvement as a way of life. Rather than figuring out how to satisfy their bosses, they focus on ways to do their jobs incrementally better.

The effectiveness of continuous improvement is underscored by the success at one of the divisions within the

Tech Group which had set as its goal breaking the one-million-dollar-a-month shipping barrier. The division got close, but just couldn't get "over the wall." In a traditional environment, management would have dictated people to make repeated assaults at the wall until they leapt over it or broke through it.

Under Tech's continual improvement program, people were able to back off and analyze the problem. What they discovered was that they were getting caught up in the typical end-of-the-month shipping "binge" that so many companies must go through to meet requisite numbers. So they started paying more attention to the problem on a daily basis, focusing on continuous improvements in scheduling, lowering inventories and evaluating all components of the shipping process. During the next quarter, the division found it could easily hit the target figure and provide more consistent service to customers.

Most problems can be addressed in a similar fashion. This entails stepping back, breaking down the problem into component parts, and then making gradual and continuous improvements in each area.

The Quality Perspective

Quality, more than any other issue, requires complete support by the company's leaders. That's because quality pervades every aspect of business, from the way the grounds are maintained to the maintenance of multi-million dollar accounts. In short, quality must become a *way of life* for everyone in the company. How does the leader show his or her commitment to such global efforts, to a Total Quality environment? Primarily by recognizing the efforts of others.

Acknowledgments for quality performance should be done in a meaningful way. At the Tech Group, for example, the President's Forum is an effective way of rewarding those who have done an exceptional job at improving quality. And at Milliken & Company, the nation's largest textile operation, "Sharing Rallies" have become a key motivational tool. "Sharing Rallies" are forums in which associates communicate ideas for improvement. They last for two days and are held every quarter. Two hundred and fifty associates are chosen to attend the rally for their excellent ideas, and of these, fifty associates are selected to present their ideas. Among those who attend the rallies are Milliken's president, Tom Malone, and chairman, Roger Milliken. Both leaders have attended every single rally since the program was first implemented eight years ago. Now that's commitment from the top!

Such buy-in from the company's leadership can never be replaced by material rewards, especially money. Monetary rewards actually turn out to be counterproductive because they encourage people to operate by themselves. A Total Quality environment must be based on a team effort, on the premise that great things are rarely done in an organization by single individuals. Recognition must flow through the company to *all* individuals who put their pride and creativity on the line.

Quality as a Means of Gaining the Competitive Edge

Breakthrough products and services may rule the roost for a while, but as competitors join the scene and markets mature, companies must differentiate themselves if they are to succeed. Quality is often the means of giving a product or service the necessary twist. In some cases, boosting quality in the conventional sense of the term—a better, more complete, more polished mousetrap—may provide the answer.

For example, Oster Communications' first newsletter, *ProFarmer*, was produced on high-gloss paper and was mailed first-class. Every other newsletter in the field looked typewritten on cheap paper and mailed third-class so it was usually out of date. The content of *ProFarmer* was pitched at a higher level, too. It was more thoughtful than its competitors and better written. Oster Communications was able to charge $50 a year, defying the "common knowledge" that farmers won't pay for information in a marketplace swimming with free information.

The Tech Group was able to provide better customer service because it focused on details, making small improvements that translated into major performance gains.

If you're looking for a way to break out of a rut or get ahead of the pack, think about continually improving quality and eliminating waste as potential means of gaining a strategic edge. For a large scale, multi-division organization, a major quality program will probably require an outside expert to develop a curriculum. For smaller scale operations, quality can begin just by getting people to think in terms of enhancing existing products, cutting waste and striving for ever better performance.

Quality, in the final analysis, is a state of mind. Act like you think, walk like you talk, and quality really can become a cornerstone of a clear-sighted organization.

*   *   *

HANDS ON

Quality Inspection

The road to quality begins with a commitment to change. Once that commitment is made, leaders must identify areas of opportunity and areas in need of improvement. Try to do this yourself by answering the following kinds of questions:

- What can we do to add value to our product or service? Can we give it a "richer" look and feel (if that's appropriate for your market)? Can we make it easier to use? Easier to service? More long-lasting? More upgradeable or expandable? How can we invest more brainpower into understanding what our customers really want?

- What are the obvious sources of waste in our company? What can we do about them? What are the subtle or hidden sources of waste that siphon off valuable cash and energy but don't add anything to our product or service? How can we eliminate these "money sinks"?

- How can we improve our manufacturing or service delivery process? Where are we today, and where do we want to be tomorrow? What's a realistic rate of improvement?

- How can we manage the cultural change necessary to bring about the continual improvement process? What can we do to change attitudes?

THE NEW ORGANIZATION CHART

To get new customers has a price, but to keep
satisfied customers is almost without cost.
On the other hand, it costs a small fortune
to get dissatisfied customers back.
— Jan Carlzon

Beyond the Arms-Length Relationship

As I travel the world picking up business concepts from other CEOs, I frequently make long-time friends with a person who has the ability to lead my thinking.

I first met Bill Benskin, Jr., as a supplier. He was the low bidder. I later met him as a fellow member of the Iowa Young Presidents Organization (YPO), where I got a close look at how customer responsiveness revolutionized his Des Moines, Iowa printing business. Bill's idea is no flash-in-the-pan. He has successfully tied his customers to him in a way that benefits everyone. I have learned a lot about customer orientation from my association with Bill.

"Originally, The Printer, Inc. was a typical job shop

operation," explains my friend Bill, the company's president. "If we put in the lowest bid, we got the job. Simple as that."

But that was back in the days when Benskin's family-owned business had two employees. Today, The Printer, Inc. has more than a hundred employees and has gone far beyond the job shop mode; it's one of the nation's leading "database" publishing companies. This means it can take data from a customer's computer and use it to print up business cards, letterhead stationery, invoices, newsletters and other printed matter. Insurance companies, for example, use The Printer, Inc. to produce business cards and forms for their armies of agents.

What's unique about database publishing is that it's virtually a paperless connection with the customer; rather than submitting purchase orders, specifications and other transmittal forms typically used in printing, customers of The Printer, Inc. place orders directly from their computer. From there, the order is printed and shipped, without any of the conventional dialogue (and chances for error) that normally accompany a print job.

What sparked the idea for this unusual approach to printing? "About three years ago we stopped talking about price and started talking about service," says Benskin. "We really wanted to eliminate duplicate efforts that typically exist between a customer and a supplier — typing out purchase orders, typing up specs, etc. If a company has 1,000 agents, why place 1,000 orders for printed materials? Why not take advantage of the economies offered by direct communication through the computer? When I started thinking about how we could link with customers, I realized that we were no longer just a printer — we were part of a team."

This was an important insight, because it allowed Benskin to understand that he was still a printing operation at heart, but his competitive advantage was the special partnership he had with his customers. "We sit down with our customers and they open up the insides of their company," he explains. "For the system to be effective, they must provide us with information about credit holds and other sensitive issues."

This requires a special element of trust. "We've gone beyond the typical arms-length relationship to the 'arms-around' relationship," says Benskin with a chuckle. "Everyone opens their doors. The customer can look into our company through a terminal and know exactly where his order is. He has total access."

According to Bill, the instant access ultimately improves the service that his customers provide to *their* "customers"—the agents, salespeople and other representatives who require printed matter. Thinking in these terms actually enabled Benskin to expand the definition of a "customer" in his own company.

Says Bill, "The typical company thinks of the customer as the guy paying the bill. You also have this attitude on the shop floor. But in fact, each group of people involved with the production process is really a customer of each other. Take our pre-press department—their customer is the press room. And the press room's customer? It's the bindery. Each person must view the next person in the process as a key account. For our product to be top notch, the press room must treat the bindery in the same way it treats *Better Homes & Gardens* or any other customer."

Bill admits that although the ideas made sense, changing the course of The Printer, Inc. took some doing: "At first, people were upset that we were buying computers instead of cameras and spending so much money on programming. It wasn't until we landed a few very large contracts that people began to realize it was the database publishing that was actually bringing in the work. This became apparent when the system went down and the customers really began to scream. It was the level of the screaming that made people aware that database publishing was really the core of the business. Too bad it took a negative event to get the idea across."

Once people at The Printer, Inc. recognized the nature of their business, Bill's next job was to change the culture of the company, a task that was accomplished largely through education and communication. Recalls Bill, "The educational effort meant we had to get through to *everyone* — not just department heads and managers. We wanted to end up with a set of teams that cuts across departments and conventional boundaries."

As important as the educational effort was, Bill is adamant that the motivation to learn and change must start at the top with executive vision. "People often ask me how my vision for the company has changed over the years. I usually answer by saying that 'No longer do I have a goal of achieving X million in sales. I've come to realize that I'm very fortunate. I don't have to report to any stockholders, so I don't have to reduce R&D or education to help next year's profits.'"

Equally significant, Bill says he's given up thinking in terms of quarterly performance. "I'm looking at three to five years," he says with determination. "I'm in this for life."

*   *   *

Caring at the Top

Without customers, you have no business. As simple as that assertion may be, it's something that companies too often forget. For some, the customer is seen as just a face on the other side of the counter or a means to a profit. Even worse, some companies view customers as necessary evils or adversaries who can be tamed with patronizing and hollow slogans like "The customer is king" or "The customer is number 1."

Yes, the customer should be treated like a king and, in truth, the customer is the number-one concern of a company. But if you think of customers merely as consumers of your product or services, then the next impulse is to find ways to cut corners by asking, "What's the least level of service we can provide and still make our targets?" This, of course, is the antithesis of the servant's attitude that is so vital to long-lasting success.

If you want to treat customers as the most important people in the world, the feeling must come from your heart. It must reflect the servant's attitude in its purest form. From the perspective of the servant, the question is never, "How much product can I get my customers to gobble up?" but rather, "How can I use my God-given creativity to find ways of fulfilling my customers' needs? How can I help my customers become happier, more profitable and more efficient?"

As discussed earlier in this book, the impulse to serve must start at the top with the leader's clear-sighted vision. It follows, then, that leaders should be in contact with customers as much as possible. If CEOs were to go out and sell their companies' products at least part of the time, they'd have a much better sense of whether or not customers are being well served by the firm. This is because when you're out there selling face-to-face with the customer, there's no place to hide—everything shows, warts and all.

A leader's direct involvement with customers occurs every day in small organizations. But when an organization gets too large, the leader often becomes removed from the front lines and loses sight of what is really happening. This doesn't have to be the case, though. Even in a big organization, top leaders can still find ways to get the customer's perspective. If you run an international airline, randomly pose as a traveler and sample your own service. If you run a consumer products conglomerate, spend a certain amount of time each week taking customer service calls and find out just what customers are actually thinking. This approach is a major step in the right direction and can help a large corporation be more responsive to its customers' needs.

Responding to Real Customer Needs: The Caring Company

Too often people assume that they know what their customers really want and that the marketplace will behave according to a monthly forecast. When that happens, the forecast takes on a reality of its own, and people begin to believe that the projections will become reality simply because they're on paper. At the end of the forecasting period when the results are in, these companies wonder why customers didn't buy according to the plan.

This often leads to destructive finger pointing in which salespeople blame their marketing counterparts for not running a good enough or timely enough campaign. People from marketing turn around and blame their peers in the engineering departments for not having new designs ready. The engineering people then blame their colleagues in purchasing or manufacturing, and so on.

In the end, management comes down and threatens reprisals if people don't boost sales. Alternately, an edict might be issued to slash costs in order to compensate for sagging sales. This in turn often robs the company of the vital resources it needs to compete over the long haul, and a vicious cycle ensues, cascading the company on a downward spiral.

Most companies approach needs in a very narrow sense: The customer needs or wants X to achieve Y—give him the X and he'll be happy as a clam. Would that the world of marketing were so simple; every company would be a terrific success!

In reality, though, customer needs go well beyond the immediate desire for the product or service to fulfill a certain function. Customers want to be shown that your company cares about them from the moment they make an inquiry to the moment they're ready to move on to a more sophisticated product or service.

Think back to Lewis Timberlake's comment in chapter 4 that people have a fundamental need to be loved. This applies to customers as well as employees. And the degree to which your company cares is reflected in everything from your sales literature and technical support to the way that your people answer the phone.

Caring for customers means that you create an environment that would be good enough for your own family. How many times have you walked into a store or an office and wondered if the founder or head of the company would shop or want to work there?

The leaders of Giant Food, a supermarket chain, answer that question every year around Thanksgiving and Christmas. They sponsor a "white glove inspection" called "Company's Coming," in which store managers and personnel are rewarded for their efforts to create a sparkling clean store for holiday shoppers. Some 20,000 people participate in the campaign, which strengthens unity throughout the company. But the real beneficiaries of the effort are the customers, who can count on walking into a crisp and clean place to shop.

Caring for customers also means going the extra mile. A west-coast department store chain, Nordstrom, goes all out by offering a remarkable selection of quality goods. Live music from a piano in one corner of the store makes shopping a pleasurable experience. Courtesy phones are almost everywhere, supplementing the store's army of knowledgeable and considerate sales people and customer service reps. No wonder that Nordstrom is gaining popularity.

And caring means putting yourself on the line for the customer whenever he or she needs help. Even giant corporations like IBM can create a caring culture in which customers remain the single most important concern. Big Blue may be one of the largest computer makers in the world, but it recognizes that it owes its success to satisfied customers. Staffers at IBM are expected to drop everything to help a customer; in fact, it is even acceptable to break an appointment with the chairman of the board if a customer is in need!

Caring is reflected in subtle and intangible ways, too. Stop and consider the ease with which people can interpret your statements and invoices. A well-laid-out statement or invoice says that you care about your customers' time and level of frustration. A statement that can be interpreted only by a post-doctoral fellow in mathematics says that you don't really care about your customers after the sale.

Your telephone routing system also reveals a lot about whether your company cares about making life easier for its customers. If customers can easily get assistance from knowledgeable people, whether they're seeking pre-sales information, technical support or accounting help, then you have a piece of a caring culture. If customers have to pass through fourteen departments to get to the party they're seeking, then you're revealing your real thoughts about customer satisfaction.

Interestingly, the computer manufacturer with the lowest customer satisfaction rating in the industry has more than *thirty* different 800 numbers that customers can call for assistance. While 800 numbers are a nice amenity, no one wants to spend half a day dialing them up just to get help.

Even the way labels are affixed on a brochure or envelope says something about whether you respect and care for your customers. What's your first reaction when you receive material or a package with a lopsided mailing label? If you're like most people, it's probably, "These people are treating me like I'm just an empty name on a mailing list." This, of course, simply expedites your mailing to the local dump or paper shredder and undermines your efforts to build lasting bonds of loyalty.

Such little things ultimately undermine all your other efforts to satisfy customers. That's why customer satisfaction is *everybody's* business, regardless of job description. Companies that off-load customer satisfaction to a complaint or customer service department are missing the boat. You can't make a poor-quality product or allow an unpleasant environment to fester and expect a division of the company to compensate for the lack of caring. Total satisfaction comes from a total company effort.

The impetus to create a caring company must begin at the top with vision-driven leadership and filter down throughout the organization. If the vision is filled with a deep desire to serve one's fellowman, it will result in a company that cares deeply about its customers. Some characteristics of a caring company are described in the next section.

What Makes a Caring Company Tick

Companies with caring attitudes can be found in all industries. Many are small or growing, others are large, yet retain an entrepreneurial passion for the person. As different as they might be, they do share a number of common traits that single them out from the pack.

Caring companies attract quality people who can catch the vision. Companies with a visionary, nurturing culture take the time to explain the big picture to their associates. They communicate the driving force that gets people excited about being in business. This vision-driven approach to motivation gives business associates the choice of attaching themselves to the boundless vision or limiting themselves to a smaller view that is job-description oriented. When business associates see themselves as being vital to improving the welfare of the customer's family, they're more inclined to answer the phone at one minute past five and stay there until the customer is satisfied.

They nurture self-fulfilled employees. You can't be compassionate with others if you're not compassionate with yourself. The same holds true of the people in an organization. If people don't feel a deep sense of respect and devotion for their company, how can they possibly experience the yearning to serve that builds bonds of loyalty with customers? Caring companies are deeply committed to their employees' physical, emotional and spiritual well-being. Their employees become likewise committed and will go to extraordinary lengths to look out for their customers' best interests.

They practice showing love. In the words of Jan Carlzon, president and CEO of Scandinavian Airlines System Group, "If I had only one management rule to give to everyone, it would be the golden rule: 'Do unto others as you would have them do unto you.' "

The caring company goes the extra mile for its business associates; they, in turn, go the extra mile for customers. And customers respond by going the extra mile in terms of loyalty to the company. In the end, everyone wins. A caring company practices in many ways an attitude of giving to, rather than taking from, its business associates, customers and suppliers.

Caring companies take risks and sometimes fail. Caring companies can afford to take risks without fear. That's because their people know that if they take chances and try something that doesn't work, they won't be punished. They're encouraged to keep trying new ideas until they find new ways of doing things. Caring companies teach people to fail and to learn from their failures.

As Jan Carlzon points out, "In my experience, there are two great motivators in life. One is fear. The other is love. You can manage an organization by fear, but if you do you will ensure that people don't perform up to their real capabilities. A person who is afraid doesn't dare perform to the limits of his or her capabilities."

They consider customers to be family. Caring companies fold customers into their organizational charts. They see them as members of an extended family, rather than faces on the other side of the counter. When customers have the good fortune to link up with caring companies, they sense the genuine warmth and concern every time they pick up the phone, talk with a sales rep or request some kind of assistance. Caring companies respond to customer needs immediately.

They take a long-term view. The key to developing a caring attitude is to treat people as customers for life, rather than one-shot consumers who may or may not be back tomorrow. Repeat business is the life-blood of any company, and customers for life are a guarantee of ongoing success.

Organizational Support

The best of intentions to create a caring company will be frustrated unless the organization is aligned to support the efforts of its business associates. For example, a company might have a very attractive product or service and excellent technical support. But at the same time, its credit policy may not be as attractive as that of its competitors. Such a company is therefore not aligned to support deep customer satisfaction.

Similarly, a company might offer an excellent line of goods. The quality is superb, the pricing is competitive, the support is very good and the credit policy is more favorable than the industry standard. Unfortunately, the company's distribution system is outdated and unreliable, so that customers frequently have to wait for unacceptable lengths of time to get their orders. This company, like the first, is not properly aligned to take advantage of its strengths and provide the best possible customer service.

The above examples are hypothetical, but they are all too representative of many companies today. To provide high-level customer service, *all* divisions and departments within an organization must work together toward a common goal. Each must see itself as a link in a chain rather than an isolated and autonomous unit.

While the concept of working in concert makes intuitive sense, it is sometimes difficult to put into practice, especially in organizations where people are rewarded for acting as "loose cannons." Take a typical manufacturing company. The sales force receives commissions on booked orders, and the production arm is rated on whether it ships orders out the door on time. Let's say that a customer of such a company places an order that consists of five components, and expects shipment within four weeks, as the sales rep promised. Two days after the order is placed, the manufacturing division informs the sales rep that one of the items will have to come from a separate division and will require an additional six weeks.

What will most likely happen in this situation? The

production department will probably not want to wait six weeks for the odd component to arrive. Rather, it would prefer to make its shipping schedule, as called for by the original order. That way it can point to the manufacturing division if the customer screams. Similarly, the sales rep will likely walk into the customer's office with four-fifths of an order so he can receive his commission in four weeks, rather than in ten weeks. But what about the customer? He's stuck with four-fifths of a functioning system, which is worthless for another month-and-a-half.

If this sounds far-fetched, it happens in one form or another every day. The details might change. But the core problem remains the same; the organization doesn't provide its people with any incentive for pulling together. The solutions to the problem are manyfold. They might involve revamping the reward system, perhaps tying bonuses and commissions into customer satisfaction ratings rather than orders placed.

The solution might entail a company-wide education program designed to replace internal competition with a sense of teamwork. As Bill Benskin pointed out, his company began to function like a smooth machine when each division began treating the division downline as a customer in its own right.

They might involve the use of sales and operations planning, in which top managers from each department get together each month to discuss anticipated customer demand and determine how the company will meet it. As demand changes because of fluctuations in exchange rates, the introduction of new technologies, etc., the company can adjust its production schedule to ensure that customers have the product they want in a timely fashion.

Each company, of course, must develop appropriate means for getting people to operate in a holistic sense. When this happens, the organization becomes more than the sum of its parts; it becomes a fine-tuned mechanism for attracting and keeping customers for life.

Beyond Customer Service: Customer Synergy

Customers for life are really partners in your business. When you have a problem, they'll stand by your side. When a competitor woos them with a tantalizing price incentive, they'll stick with you because you're fulfilling the full spectrum of their needs. When you have a new idea, they'll give you a reality check.

The last point is extremely important, perhaps the most important, because it hints at the synergistic nature of the company-customer relationship. Customer partnerships provide a unique opportunity to test new ideas in a small or growing company. And new ideas are the hope for any business's future.

When customers enter into an unspoken partnership with your company, your people can use them as sounding boards for creative ideas that may lead to new products and services. Customer feedback can save you tremendous amounts of time and money and help you avoid devastating mistakes. This differs from traditional market testing in that the customers truly participate in the birth and development of a new idea. Such ownership further reinforces the bonds of loyalty between company and the customer because people generally enjoy having a sense of ownership in the products they buy and use.

A good example of this occurred at Oster Communications when the Research and Development group decided it would get new ideas for FutureSource, a real-time futures price quote, news and technical analysis service for people who use futures markets to lay off risk. The R&D team sat in on customer focus groups, attended seminars with customers and developed friendships with several of them.

This open line of communication through the company's customers and customer service department put the Product Development people on the very cutting edge of the field. As a result, the group developed a product that took the industry by surprise because it delivered a higher quality product on a personal computer than many competitors were able to deliver on a mini- or mainframe computer.

Over a three-year period, growth in that product line doubled from $4.5 million to $9 million. The customer got more for his money, and the FutureSource division of the company was recognized as a leader in the industry. That, of course, had a tremendous impact on morale as well.

As you can see, this synergy between customer and company can be a valuable way to translate new ideas into reality and to avoid costly mistakes. Customer synergy has one added benefit; it's self-generating. Once customers realize that they can play a direct role in shaping new products and service, they'll tend to come up with ideas of their own and bring them to you for development.

In some industries, such as software, this can actually lead to a joint venture in which the software you create for a customer becomes a more generic product. With a variety of licensing and royalty arrangements, both parties can profit handsomely from such collaborative efforts.

Finally, the very presence of customer synergy is a good indicator that you've broken down the traditional wall that has separated companies and their customers for too long. Customer synergy elevates your company to a higher plane of business that is based on trust and caring. When those feelings prevail, everyone comes out a winner.

* * *

HANDS ON

An organization is only as strong as its weakest link. To deliver the best quality customer service, it's therefore necessary to identify where your company excels and where it needs bolstering. One way to do this is to imagine yourself as a customer of your own company. Ask yourself the following questions. (If you don't know the answers, talk to your department or division heads. You might also want to ask yourself *why* you don't know the answers. You might learn a lot about your own leadership style!)

- How quickly could you get pre-sales information about a product or service?

- How accurate would the information be? How difficult would it be to discuss pre-sales questions with a customer support or sales rep?

- What would the ordering process be like? Would the salespeople be efficient and courteous? Knowledgeable? How long would the ordering process take?

- Would the product arrive or the service begin in a timely way?

- What would happen if the product were damaged or the service incomplete? Would it be obvious who you should call? How long would it take before help arrived?

- How difficult would it be to get ongoing support once the product or service was up and running? Is the support line clearly identified in your product literature? Did the sales rep make it clear who you should call? How long did you have to wait before actually getting through to the right party? If you reached a recorded message, how long would it take before someone got back to you?

- How easy would it be to alter or upgrade to a different product or service line?

- All in all, would you buy from your company again? If not, what needs the most fixing? How would you go about correcting the deficiencies? If so, what are your company's overwhelming positive attributes? How could you make the company even stronger?

THE SUPPLIER
CONNECTION

*Great things are done when men and mountains
meet; this is not done by jostling in the street.*
— William Blake, **Notebook**

Suppliers for Life . . .

You can't talk business with Stew Leonard for more
than ten minutes before he launches into some great customer or supplier story. Stew is an excellent student of the
people he buys from and the customers he serves. By
responding to the "lessons of the marketplace," Stew and
his family have become one of the most talked about grocers
in America.

Christmas 1988 was a special one for Stew Leonard,
president of Stew Leonard's, the world's largest dairy store.
The company sold 25,000 Christmas trees, making it a
banner year. Then, in the middle of January, Stew got a
phone call from one of his suppliers, the owner of a small
Canadian farm. A number of the supplier's trees had gotten
damaged en route and were unsalable. The trucking company refused to take any responsibility, so the supplier,
whose margins were low to begin with, faced a loss on the
sale. He decided to see if Leonard might help out.

"The vendor asked if I'd consider splitting the loss with him," Stew explains. "It was a little over $2,000. I said to myself, 'This guy sent us the most beautiful Christmas trees we've ever seen. How could I let him take a loss?' So I said, 'Sure . . . be glad to.' And he said, 'Boy, am I looking forward to doing business with you next year!' I said, 'Same for me!' I didn't make as much money, but I guarantee you one thing: He'll be a supplier for life."

Stew's attitude is pretty different from the way business is usually conducted. Says Leonard, "In the old days, customers would expect the suppliers to change their attitude before they change theirs. Today, customers are smart enough to realize that the suppliers can be a valuable asset, so they've begun developing a relationship with them."

This closeness doesn't mean that price negotiation doesn't go on. "We still want to get the best deal," Stew notes, "as long as it works for the supplier, too. So we may not always get the very best price. But instead we get someone who will be in it for the long haul. Most of the suppliers we go with have been around for years and years. That way we don't need any inspection people at the docks — we trust our suppliers to give us their best."

The key, according to Stew, is the site visit: "We visit all new suppliers so we can see firsthand the supplier's pride in the product. Anyone who produces a great product will have more pride than his competitors. If you're in a gridlock situation about choosing suppliers, go visit them. Let them show off; let them impress you. What I find is that when you go, you'll usually break the gridlock."

"When we visit a site we also want to negotiate a fair price," he continues. "But equally important, we want to develop a friendship. That means sitting down and breaking bread with the person. That means meeting the people who do the billing so if there's a problem we can call up and say, 'Hey, Charlie, or hey, Sue, I need some help with this invoice . . . ' When we leave, we want an element of mutual trust. You can't do business without that trust."

Another benefit of going to visit suppliers is that you often get new ideas for solving old problems. "We had a problem with an egg farmer," recalls Leonard. "We couldn't negotiate the price down to a point that worked for both of us. So we went and visited his farm and found that he was bringing eggs in from the chicken house in flats. He had a crew of people taking eggs off flats and then packaging them, so he had a whole extra step. We said, 'How about sending the eggs in flats? That will cut your costs and you can pass some savings along to us.' He agreed right away."

There's a second part of the egg story, too. As Stew explains, a close relationship with a vendor leads to mutual problem-solving efforts: "When we got the eggs in flats, we had to unpack them and transfer them to metal cases. So we asked the egg farmer if he could find an economical way to ship the eggs in metal cases for us. He researched the situation and presto! The eggs started coming in metal cases rather than cardboard boxes."

For Stew Leonard, the bottom line in dealing with suppliers is very simple. "I won't buy from anybody I don't like," he admits with pride. "I think that's really important because you're not just going into a paper deal, you're entering into a relationship. As soon as I shake hands with a supplier, I sit there and hold hands for a minute and say, 'Look, no matter what we've talked about and promised, problems will come up. The real agreement here is that we're going to work out problems together.' Our mission is to have happy customers at a profit if we can, at a loss if we must, but always happy customers. And suppliers play a big part in making our mission work."

*   *   *

Supplier Alliances

As Stew Leonard points out, companies traditionally
looked at suppliers solely in terms of the best deal. Smart
purchasing meant pitting one supplier against the other to
drive the price down. And if a supplier went broke as a
result of getting hammered continually? No problem—just
go out and find another one. After all, there are plenty of
suppliers just dying to get new business.

Today that kind of thinking is being replaced with a
new win-win attitude in which suppliers are regarded as
part of the team. Value-based companies know that it is
unethical to consider their company's well-being more important than the well-being of their suppliers. They also
recognize the immense strategic gains to be had by viewing
suppliers as partners.

In fact, "supplier alliances" may well be the key to
survival and success in an ever-competitive global
marketplace. Who has the time to go "vendor shopping"
while other companies, who are working hand in hand with
their suppliers, are refining their products and focusing
their energies on better ways to deliver service? No one, of
course.

Supplier alliances require a fundamental change in
our understanding of how business is done. First of all, it
means reducing the number of vendors from whom you
purchase parts or service. Typically, buying companies
maintain a large vendor pool so that bids can be placed and
the lowest price can be obtained. Perhaps supplier A really
wanted the job, but supplier B, who hoped to shoe-horn
himself into your business, was willing to break even or
even take a slight loss.

Supplier B thought he was taking a long-term view.

But in fact, supplier A might use the same tactic on the next round, just to regain the business. At this point, the buying company has gotten so used to rock-bottom prices that it expects pricing that no vendor can afford to offer on a sustained basis. So perhaps suppliers A and B drop out of the race while supplier C or D or E takes a crack at the opportunity.

With enlightened buying practices, there's no need for a large buyer pool. Here's why. The company first selects a few suppliers for each part or service it needs. The selection is based on the vendor's ability to deliver quality and offer advanced technical capabilities. The question becomes: Who can consistently give us the best product? Who can help us solve problems? Who can help us innovate new products and services for our own customers? In short, who will be responsive enough to be our partners?

The next step is pricing. If the buying company has adopted quality techniques such as "Just-in-Time" (chapter 5), it will request material in smaller batches and have it delivered more frequently. This flies in the face of the traditional volume concept of "buy more, pay less," so a compromise has to be reached. The company cannot expect the same kind of pricing it could obtain by setting vendors at each others' throats. But it must also realize the enormous benefits it will gain from not having to spend time fighting with vendors and from consistently receiving higher quality materials.

On the flip side of the coin, the supplier must realize that even though his customer might be placing smaller orders, the loss in economy will be offset by the guarantee of long-term business. In other words, the buying company and supplier must arrive at a *fair* price.

If this concept seems foreign to the American way of doing business, it in fact is. The supplier alliance concept is born out of the Japanese concept of Just-in-Time. As described in chapter 5, Just-in-Time requires that parts are delivered as they are needed. This means that vendors cannot afford to deliver defective material; otherwise, the whole process gets jarred. But you can't expect suppliers to achieve a zero-defect state unless you work closely with them.

Herein lies the crux of the supplier alliance: By dealing with a very limited number of suppliers (generally a primary and an alternate in case the primary supplier has an unexpected problem), you can focus your attention on educating them and helping them improve so they can give you better service. How much reduction is possible? Xerox, one of the most successful Just-in-Time companies in America, has been able to reduce its supplier pool from more than 3,000 to about 300. Even a company of Xerox's size can't work closely with 3,000 suppliers; by comparison, 300 is a breeze.

At Oster Communications, we have a printer who has served us well since our first day in business. Congdon Printing is just a block away. With certain newsletters that require quick turnaround, it's important that we have access to a press—and we don't want to own one.

A memo from Rich Congdon to some of his new associates expresses his world-class philosophy which helps keep both organizations in business:

> It is no secret that Oster Communications is Congdon Printing Company's number-one customer. *Pro-Farmer* is the only customer that enjoys "next on press" job status. This commitment is long-standing and will not change, even though at times it has put our business relationships with some other customers in jeopardy.
>
> Congdon Printing Company is always concerned about being competitive. However, we realize that price alone is not the only measure of value. Our prices will

never be so low that we must compromise our commitment to Oster's "next on press" status.

We are recommitting ourselves to providing products printed correctly, on time and at competitive prices. We will work with Oster to find ways to meet their needs. Our past history has demonstrated Congdon's willingness to be there when Oster needed us for quick turnarounds and quality pieces. Congdon's has also demonstrated our commitment to be innovative and responsive to procedures and equipment to meet Oster's needs.

Spend time helping your suppliers grow rather than cutting the "best deal," and you'll cultivate relationships that will pay off handsomely in the long run.

Stew Leonard helped one of his Christmas tree suppliers in a very fundamental way—through his bank account. Sharing a "hit" is one way that buying companies can help their suppliers out of a jam. Another way is to provide technical assistance. Many progressive companies actually give their suppliers technical support in order to help them cut costs and achieve higher levels of quality.

Working with suppliers also means sharing more information about your own needs. If you're working with a select group of suppliers, you can afford to open your company to them in the way that Bill Benskin describes in chapter 7. Obviously, you can do this only with people whom you trust as partners. In larger companies, this element of openness leads to tremendous efficiencies; buying companies can place orders electronically in a supplier's system, eliminating the wasteful duplication of energy and paperwork.

Even on a smaller scale, where the electronic sharing of information may not be possible or economically feasible, it still makes sense to share your projected quarterly or annual needs with suppliers so they can plan accordingly.

This will help them do a better job of projecting their own cash flows and taking whatever actions are necessary to achieve their revenue needs. And the healthier the supplier's company, the better the service he can provide to you.

Working with suppliers also means actively bringing them into the development process. Too often, suppliers are regarded as "black boxes": You hand them a set of specifications and expect a finished product in return. If suppliers are involved during the planning stages, they can often help you avoid products or services that will be expensive to make or deliver in the long run.

That's another reason it's important to pick vendors who have enough technical savvy to give you feedback about your current and future products. Again, this is the essence of the supplier alliance and the partnership approach to doing business.

Finally, suppliers can provide you with unique observations about the marketplace and the industry. Without compromising other customers' confidentiality, they can teach you about new techniques and technologies as well as new approaches to satisfying customers. This, of course, is another reason you want to choose suppliers who understand the marketplace and are on the leading edge of their fields. Suppliers, like your sales force and service force, are ways of multiplying your eyes and ears.

*   *   *

HANDS ON

Supplier Check

Following Stew Leonard's lead, think in terms of "suppliers for life." To do so means that you must pick and choose your suppliers very carefully. Use the following checklist* to see how your current vendors stack up. Then use it to evaluate suppliers who could be with you over the long haul.

1. Are they willing to take a long-term view?

2. Do your vendors consistently produce quality goods?

3. Will they go the extra mile when you need help?

4. Are they willing to learn from you so they can meet your specifications?

5. Do they have the technical savvy to help you add further value to your current product lines?

6. Do they offer useful hints and suggestions or wait until you solicit their advice?

7. Do they have the same attitude about your customers as you do?

8. Would you want to break bread with them?

---

*There are many technical measures for selecting and working with vendors. A complete list would be beyond the scope of this book. For an exhaustive discussion of the vendor selection process, see John Schorr's *High Performance Purchasing* (published by the Oliver Wight Company).

THE COMPETITOR PERSPECTIVE

People are always blaming their circumstances for what they are. I don't believe in circumstances. The people who get on in this world are the people who get up and look for the circumstances they want, and, if they can't find them, make them.

—George Bernard Shaw

Succeeding Through Niches

Christopher Crane is a former vice president of Oster Communications. As a member of our advisory board, he helps me think about competing in a global communications market. His win-win thinking may stimulate some ideas that will help your organization find a fit so it can grow faster.

"The budget segment of the women's clothing business is highly competitive," states Chris, who is group division president of Beeba's Creations, a $125 million-a-year women's clothing operation. "The traditional approach to our business is generally to undercut competitors' prices. A retailer will come to us for a product and then go to my competitors. He'll seek a price quote on delivering 6,000 units by a certain time, so price really is the first criterion for getting an order."

Given this situation, Chris finds it extremely difficult to compete with smaller companies that operate on low overhead, especially small family operations in India, Bangladesh and other developing countries. While these companies don't offer much in the way of designer goods, they can outcompete Beeba's on smaller orders.

The solution? Chris relies on his company's strengths rather than fighting battles he can't win. "One of the tenets of our mission statement," he says, "is to be a major wholesaler to major retailers. We have the capabilities to serve the largest retailers. The consolidation that has occurred in the industry has resulted in fewer but larger retailers who need large vendors like Beeba's. When Wal-Mart wants 300,000 units, the smaller overseas companies can't possibly deliver. We can, so that's where we position ourselves."

Despite the nature of his business, Chris believes that competing solely on the basis of price leaves you very vulnerable. "It's so easy for competitors to take away your business with a minimum of effort. The better approach is to sell *solutions* to customers and differentiate yourself by developing a distinctive competence. If you can get that through the whole company, you'll compete on a different plane."

When someone does try to engage you in a price war, Chris suggests that if you have the resources, meet their challenge several times. "This sends a nonverbal signal that you're willing to play their game," he says. "Hopefully, they'll give up and say, 'Let's compete on another basis.' When they do so, it's possible for more competitors to participate in the market."

"At Beeba's," Chris continues, "we looked around and

saw there were few wholesalers with capital. Thus our $43 million in net worth makes us far stronger financially than the great majority of our competitors. The ability to finance 'mega-orders' is a key competitive edge. We also have enormous production capacity relative to our competitors. Therefore we do not focus on little accounts where we can't do as well as small competitors. Our vision isn't to dominate the industry, but rather to succeed by applying our strengths to market opportunities."

While Chris prefers indirect competition to "head-bashing," he admits that in some cases it's not possible for everyone to find a niche and succeed. Says Chris, "Some competitors don't work hard enough or smart enough. Some make mistakes like taking on too much debt, and some just get whipsawed later in difficult economic times. Others fail to identify key trends in their industry and are relegated to non-viable positions. This is hackneyed, but it's true. The railroads decided that they were in the railroad business, not in the transportation business. If they'd taken a broader view, they wouldn't have lost out to interstate trucking or the airlines."

Nevertheless, Chris believes that most reasonably good players can win. "They do it by either intuitively or formally looking at the threats and opportunities in the marketplace and then examining their own strengths and weaknesses. This underlies a core strategy that guides them in the competitive arena," he comments.

When you view the marketplace from this perspective, Chris believes that competition becomes a wonderful mechanism that ultimately serves people. "It fosters lower prices, more innovations and better services," he insists. "It creates niches in which industry players offer specialized goods and services, so that the whole market is well served. When that happens, customers and competitors benefit alike."

*   *   *

Styles of Competing

For many people, competing in the business world conjures up images of mortal combat. This is reinforced by the scores of business books that equate doing business with doing battle. Just look at the business section of a typical bookstore and you'll find titles such as *Life and Death on the Corporate Battlefield, Marketing Warfare* and *Guerilla Marketing.*

For other people, competition isn't a "take-no-prisoners" struggle; it's a healthy sports event that stimulates growth and brings continual improvement to the marketplace. This view is nicely summed up by Gary Ginter, executive vice president of the Chicago Research and Trading Group. According to Ginter, the "zero sum gain" approach doesn't really apply to business. "God is not a 'zero sum' God," he says. "God created reality so that people can do better with their particular mix of talents, market position and capabilities. Competition is His way for man to improve man's use of skills. Winners and losers are simply aspects of doing better or worse."

The attitude that predominates in a company is an extension of the executive's vision. If the leader sees himself as a "tank commando," leading a charge into enemy territory, then everyone will be steeled up for a head-to-head fight where winner takes all and everything needed to get the job done is fair play.

If the leader's vision is based on a philosophy of live and let live, compete and grow—manifestations of the nurturing culture—people will look at competition as a stimulus for creative action. In short, healthy competition will become part of the culture's applied vision.

Unfortunately, many leaders who have worked their

way up the ranks of large corporations only know head-on competition and regard their employees as troops on active duty. In this chapter, we'll briefly look at the dangers of the combat mentality and describe numerous alternatives through which companies can compete indirectly. As Chris Crane pointed out, when this happens, everybody wins.

The Illusion of Total Victory

By definition, head-to-head combat entails casualties on both sides. Sure, one company might "win" some additional market share, but at what cost? Consider, for example, how much money gets poured into consumer product campaigns.

During the "Spaghetti Sauce Wars" of the early '80s, for example, major food processors launched brand after brand into the lucrative and growing spaghetti sauce market (valued at more than $500 million a year at the time). Although Ragu enjoyed more than a 50-percent market share, it made sure that it would not play second tomato to any competitor by dumping $60 million worth of discount coupons into the fray. *Sixty million dollars!* Sixty million dollars could have funded scores of new companies and the development of whole new lines of products, perhaps with even better long-term returns on investment than that obtained through spaghetti sauce sales.

In addition to the high cost of head-to-head combat, companies that engage in "competitor bashing" ultimately do themselves and their customers a disservice. When the announcer on a television commercial points to a competing product and flogs it for its inferior taste, features, quality or other "shortcomings," he or she is merely casting doubt on the *whole* market. And as consumers begin to think in terms of negatives, they approach products with an eye toward, "What's missing? What's this company trying to foist upon me? What's the catch?" In the end, the consuming public becomes wary of all products as it tries to wade through the truth and the hype. Everyone, then, becomes a loser.

Win-Win: The Power of Indirect Competition

Many of today's best companies achieve success by investing brainpower rather than firepower. And they do so largely by using a single principle: They *change* the playing field so that they can avoid direct confrontation whenever possible. When faced with competitors who insist on going head-to-head, they simply alter the rules or move the game to a different arena. Here are some tried and proven techniques for changing the playing field. Think about them the next time you're tempted to go head-to-head with another company.

Technique 1: Add Value Wherever Possible

The key to success is developing your own strengths. If a competitor is trying to goad you into a price-slashing war and you can't afford to lower your costs, find other ways to make your product or service worth the money. If a competitor "clones" your wares, offer better support. If a competitor matches your support, innovate and make a better mousetrap.

In other words, change the playing field so that you're no longer competing with the same product or service — while your competitor is broadcasting on AM, you've suddenly shifted to FM. No interference. And if a competitor follows suit, change the field again, finding new incentives for customers to remain loyal and for prospective customers to choose your company as their supplier.

When you think about adding value, go beyond the obvious action of adding new features. People don't buy a product or service just because it offers more. They're equally affected, and perhaps even more so, by numerous intangibles. Here are some aspects that you should consider when enhancing your product's worth:

Maintain your product information chain. Is it easy for people to learn about your products and services? Nothing is more frustrating to a potential customer than to "get the runaround" when making an initial inquiry. Conversely, nothing builds confidence like a company in which *everyone* seems to know something about the product, or can at least direct you to the right person without fumbling or guessing.

In a customer-driven company, it is understood that the first point of a potential sale is the receptionist, and that each link in the "customer information chain" is the weakest link. Once the link breaks, the customer is left dangling, and the chances of making a sale rapidly diminish.

Your sales literature is a vital aspect of the customer information chain. How effective are your brochures, pamphlets and other "collateral" pieces? Can people readily understand the benefits of your product or service, or is it all glitter and hype? People today are so bombarded with information that they have no time or patience to decipher convoluted or hidden messages.

To put this into perspective, Bell Labs recently determined that a single edition of *The New York Times* contains more new information than a sixteenth-century adult had to process in his or her entire lifetime! The point? Don't add anything unnecessary to the customer's information burden; otherwise, you may not get any consideration at all.

Make your products/service easy to understand and use. One of the biggest complaints among consumers today is that products are too complicated. Again, given the "information overload" problem, few people have the time or patience to spend hours figuring something out that should take but ten minutes if the manuals were adequate. In fact, in the world of microcomputers, hardware and software products are often condemned in the press because of inadequate manuals. How often we see a review that says something to the effect of "an otherwise excellent product, flawed by its poor documentation."

Beyond bad press, when a product is hard to use and/or poorly explained, your cost of support skyrockets. Consider the case of Hewlett-Packard's LaserJet printer. At this writing, HP receives about 20,000 calls a month at its technical support center. A good number of the calls stem from the fact that the printer is factory set to be plugged into what is called a "serial port" on the computer.

Many people, however, want to use it with their "parallel" computer port because data is transmitted faster and the software setup is easier. To switch the setting on the printer requires wading through a convoluted process that is described in the manual but not clearly enough. As a result, people often call and report that their new printer doesn't work, and HP's technical support team walks them through the setup process, which actually takes about a minute.

Wouldn't it make more sense to include a large notice on a separate sheet of paper regarding the setup issue, or to place a notice on the first page of the manual preceded by "Before You Begin . . . "? Clearly there are many opportunities to inform the customer about the potential difficulty—each of which must be less expensive than tying up valuable technical support personnel time.

The world of products and services abounds with examples like the LaserJet. And the sad part is that the solution is usually very simple: Just put yourself in the customer's shoes. At a certain point in your development cycle, you can no longer have an objective view of your product or service, and you won't be able to determine what information needs to be conveyed. Therefore, ask novices from outside the company whether they understand how to use your product or service based on the manuals or training you provide.

If you find that you're dealing with two groups of users, one inexperienced and the other experienced, provide a "two tier" instruction path that gives novices the basic training they need and advanced users the key information they need to build upon their knowledge base.

Here are some questions to ask yourself and others when you evaluate your instructional material:

- Does it presuppose any background knowledge? If so, does the material tell me where to get it?

- Does it walk me through all steps of usage, from the moment I open the box or begin the service?

- Does it contain realistic examples to illustrate the key points and put the product or service in context?

- Does it contain enough illustrations to support the text? And do the illustrations actually correspond to the product?

- Does it try to anticipate unique situations and provide scenarios to cover all bases?

- Does it provide a comprehensive table of contents or index?

- Does it have a troubleshooting section that provides solutions to the most common problems that customers encounter?

- Does it have a clearly marked section listing addresses and numbers to call for additional help?

● Does it have a glossary of terms relating to the product or service?

If you can say "yes" to all of the above questions (if relevant), you have the makings of useful instructional materials. If the writing and production quality are good, you might actually have a first-rate piece on your hands.

Even so, seek more feedback. Constantly measure your performance. In business as in sports, nothing improves without measurement. Raise the high bar a notch every time you think you've attained your goal. Although you might see only small improvements on subsequent revisions, each improvement can only strengthen your materials and provide added benefits to the customer.

By bringing customers into the loop and creating the best manuals or training in the industry, you also gain a competitive edge. Good instruction breeds confidence in the strength of your product or service and demonstrates a commitment toward serving the customer. That's something no advertising could ever hope to achieve.

Provide the best possible customer support. Even with top-notch instructional material and training, customers will inevitably need help. Some will need assistance with basic issues, while others will have unique problems related to their particular use of the product or service. Either way, you can gain a competitive advantage by providing excellent support to every customer who has a problem. If two products or services are otherwise equal, support will often be the tie-breaker.

Give people an 800 telephone number and, as your product or service grows in popularity, make sure that you have enough knowledgeable people to manage the phones. Consider the case of the number-one-selling word processing program for personal computers, WordPerfect. Aside from having the features that users clamor for, the company has achieved preeminence by offering what all industry pundits acknowledge to be the best technical support in the software business. Today, WordPerfect Corporation employs more than 300 technical support people who can be reached toll-free. Users know that they can get expert help with any problem they're experiencing. They also know that the technical support staff will be patient and courteous, giving them as much time as necessary. Today, when many fine word processing packages are available, WordPerfect's technical support program puts it clearly ahead of the pack.

Follow WordPerfect's lead and gain an edge on your competitors by offering better support to your customers. Even if your product or service may not require intensive customer assistance, be prepared to provide it. A handful of grateful customers may start a grassroots movement that catapults your company to the number one spot.

Innovate! "Innovation" might be somewhat hackneyed these days, having been the subject of many popular books and articles. But it is, nevertheless, the lifeblood of any business. Even a "mature" business where there appears to be little opportunity for creative change must innovate; no company today can afford to rest on its laurels if it wishes to survive. The competitive pressures are just too great.

Domestically, small start-up firms are cropping up throughout the country in just about every conceivable industry. Internationally, competitors in the Pacific Rim are offering high-quality, feature-laden products at unbeatable prices. And the rapid march of technology itself is creating whole new opportunities for entrepreneurs and companies to supplant existing products and services.

Innovation offers companies unique opportunities to compete in the global marketplace. And the key to succeeding with a better mousetrap is just that: Actually *make* a better mousetrap. To do so, you need to distinguish between two types of innovation: cosmetic and substantive.

Cosmetic innovation really isn't innovation at all; it's repackaging a product or service with "bells and whistles," tail fins and the like. Cosmetic change adds no inherent value to the product, and is usually recognized by customers as a company's effort to sell the same old stuff under new wraps.

Meaningful change, on the other end, makes the product or service better. If you think of products and services as solutions to customer problems, then meaningful change allows you to sell better solutions. This in turn will attract new customers and further make your existing customers immune to the overtures of competitors.

For innovation to be meaningful, it must address one or more of the following criteria:

- *Does it make the product or service more "transparent"?* In other words, does the innovation allow you to focus more on the functionality than on mechanics of the product or service? For example, the new automatic still cameras do everything except walk the film to the photo store. Because all of the settings are taken care of, people can pay more attention to composition and subject matter, rather than fidgeting with f-stop, shutter speed and focus settings.

- *Does it allow people to use the product or service more efficiently?* New wrinkles can be added to even the most stodgy products and services. Consider Arm & Hammer Baking Soda, which has been around for dozens of years. Several years ago, the manufacturer of the time-honored substance began promoting Arm & Hammer's ability to keep refrigerators smelling clean and fresh. To help people use the product more effectively in this capacity, the company added a blank chart on the back of the carton, so that people could record how long a particular box had been in use. Not a major enhancement, but a clever enough innovation to make the product more useful.

- *Does it help users save time?* In this hurried world, any feature that saves people time and energy will be seen as a compelling reason to buy one product or service over another. A good example of innovation in this area is the end-of-the-year tally provided by American Express to its card holders. One of the biggest nuisances for credit card users is to categorize and total expenditures for tax and business purposes. AMEX took all the pain out of the procedure by innovating the end-of-year management report for individual and business users. The report totals expenses by category and provides both summary and detail information, sparing users hours of time at the calculator.

- *Does it allow people to use the product or service in new ways?* In a nutshell, all of these criteria ask the same question: Does the innovation enable you to better solve your customers' problems? If the answer is "yes," you should follow through with it. If you really aren't sure, and your market tests are ambiguous, then you'd better rethink whether it's worth committing more time and resources to the effort, because someone, at some time, will offer the "real thing" and leave your offering in the dust.

Technique 2: Look for Strategic Alliances

When you engage in direct, head-to-head competition, you're going it alone. Think of how much further you can go by joining forces with other companies in a common effort. Simple strategic alliances are commonplace in the business world between companies like Renault and

American Motors, and Philips and DuPont (for making compact disks).

A more unusual type alliance occurs when a group of companies gets together and pools their resources rather than bashing their heads. One of the best examples of this is the Microelectronics and Computer Technology Corporation (MCC), a research consortium funded by Control Data, Sperry, Honeywell and other blue-chip companies, many of which are normally arch rivals. The goal of MCC was to help U.S. companies become more competitive against the incoming waves of Japanese technological breakthroughs, each of which eroded the potential for U.S. companies to retain commanding shares of the market.

By pooling their resources and brainpower and sharing the R&D results, each company could save a tremendous amount of time and energy. Control Data, one of the founding companies, invested $13 million in 1983 and several years later reaped an estimated $120 million in research benefits.

Another type of alliance is now being used by the major television networks to compete against the cable television users. As the market share for free television drops, the major networks have pondered ways of competing with the hundreds of cable stations springing up across the country. The solution? Team up with companies like K Mart, Pizza Hut, Sears and McDonald's to help promote the programming available on free television. Sears, for example, will include various advertisements in statements describing the programs available on ABC.

The networks are also encouraging Panasonic and other major VCR manufacturers to build in the ability to automatically record network stations. Again, this ease-of-use issue could give the networks an indirect edge in a highly competitive market.

To build an alliance, consider the following issues:

Will everyone come out a winner as a result of the alliance? Make a checklist of how the alliance can benefit all "stakeholders" — anyone who has an interest in the companies, including customers, employees, suppliers and the community at large. Think about the impact that your alliance will have on each stakeholder group. Evaluate the net effect before taking action.

Does the company that you plan to align with have similar interests? An alliance should be founded on the understanding that everyone will equally benefit from the resulting effort. If one partner sees the alliance as a stepping stone for getting a leg up on other partners, it won't work.

Will the alliance truly result in unique capabilities? For an alliance to work, the parties must bring complementary talents to the table. If everyone has the same skills and resources, then you're merely adding one plus one. But if the mix of skills and resources is truly complementary, then the whole will be greater than the sum of the parts. If you have tremendous R&D strengths, but don't have the marketing channels, link up with a marketing organization, not another R&D organization. The same holds for all other business development functions.

The bottom line is that alliances are like marriages. If you go in with uncertainty or dubious motives, the results can be disastrous for everyone involved. If you go in with the belief and conviction that "this is it," you may find yourself in a perpetual state of matrimonial bliss.

Technique 3: Ignore the Challenge

Sometimes the best way to avoid direct competition is to ignore it altogether. These days, for example, the many automakers at home and abroad have begun comparing their luxury cars to Mercedes-Benz. Regardless of whether or not the claims are warranted, Mercedes has a simple response to its competitors: Pretend they don't exist.

Incumbent politicians use this "ostrich" technique all the time (or at least they should). An incumbent has nothing to gain and everything to lose by responding to the goading of a contender. At worst, the contender will make the incumbent look foolish or dredge some embarrassing skeleton from a closet. At best, the incumbent will emerge without losing ground. So why risk it?

In business, the same principle holds. If a competitor goads you into responding to a challenge, don't "lower" yourself by going a few rounds in the ring — you can only lose. You lose by spending money and you lose by diverting energy from the very thing that makes your company successful: your total commitment to a superior product or service.

Instead of responding to challenges, focus your energy on your strengths. Promote the quality, uniqueness or inherent worthiness of your product. Spend your money on shoring up weaknesses and innovating new features that will give you a competitive edge.

The key point here is that a threat (i.e., a competitive attack or challenge) requires two people. If you refuse to acknowledge the threat, then it doesn't exist. It requires your participation if it is to become a reality. By keeping your nose to your own grindstone, would-be attackers will eventually disappear.

Of course, if someone is maligning your company you might want to take legal action, although this, too, can backfire if the malignment is part of a competitor's scheme to get you to pay for name or product recognition. For example, an upstart fast food chain called Big Bite attempted to goad Wendy's, McDonald's and Burger King into legal action by running ads that mocked "Little Wendy," "Ronald McDonald" and other icons of the major chains. Wendy's took the bait and sued Big Bite, winning an injunction against the ads. But Big Bite was the real winner as it garnered tens of thousands of dollars in free publicity.

The lesson? Put your ego aside when a competitor tries to engage you in all-out war. Remember, you can win without firing a shot just by being yourself.

Technique 4: Run From It

Yet another means of indirect competition is escape. There are times when a major competitor moves in and there's simply no way you can survive without committing enormous resources to a major head-to-head campaign. In these instances, you might consider applying your resources to another pursuit.

But isn't this a tremendous loss of face? It could be, if you interpret it as escape "from." If you interpret the action in terms of escape "to," you're merely seizing an opportunity to apply your creativity, talents and resources to an endeavor where they are more likely to flourish.

That's exactly what helicopter maker Kaman Corporation did during the late sixties, when it found its woodworking shops (used to make helicopter blades) idle because of a decline in defense contracts. Charles Kaman, an avid guitarist, helped solve the problem by temporarily flying away from the helicopter market and applying the company's knowledge of aerodynamics and vibration control to land in the acoustic guitar business. Kaman's line of sleek guitars, Ovation, became an instant success, and by the late seventies the company had snagged nearly three quarters of the U.S. market.

Other companies that retreated today and attacked

elsewhere tomorrow include Exxon Corp, which finally went back to the oil business after soaking in a $60 million red ink bath during its foray into office automation equipment, and Coca Cola, which sold off Wine Spectrum after discovering that selling wine is very different from selling soft drinks.

Growing Through Competition

At this point, you've seen numerous alternatives to direct, head-on competition. If your company is staffed with people who live on combat alert, it's time to send a new message: We compete on the basis of our strengths; as we build on our strengths, we improve and grow. For this clear-sighted vision to be applied on a daily basis, the leader must work with department heads or team leaders to get them thinking about what makes the company tick, why customers buy from it and how it can improve.

This can be done during special in-house roundtable meetings or during offsite retreats. Either way, your results will be most beneficial if you pass out a questionnaire to the participants, asking them to ponder the following:

1. What do we really sell? Go beyond the obvious details of our product or service and describe the customer problems that we solve. (We don't just sell information, we help farmers earn more money and achieve a better standard of living.)

2. How can we help our customers use our products and services in new ways to solve other problems? (We can help people in their marketing efforts by using their telephones as marketing instruments.)

3. How can we add value to our existing products and services? (We can make it easier for customers to trade

in their older Model 400s and receive a healthy discount on the new Model 500s.)

4. Are there niches that we can fill using our existing technologies? (Can we use our tools and dies to create a better wrench? Can we use our information database to create an on-line news service?)

5. Where are the gaps in the marketplace today? What goods and services aren't being provided by our competitors? What customer needs are going unmet? (As the high-tech economy grows, there will be a need for a specialized "high-tech yellow pages." The regional phone companies haven't seized this opportunity yet. Let's explore it ourselves.)

6. Where are our competitors focusing? (All our competitors in the health club business are competing on price. Let's change the game and offer health spas in airports and other under-served markets.)

7. Why are we unique and how can we maintain our uniqueness in an ever-more-competitive world? (We truly understand the needs of our readers, and we're known for accurate, timely information. We need to continually upgrade our technology, increase our staff, and provide new types of information that will ultimately help our readers work more productively and profitably and lead more satisfied lives.)

The easiest way to use the information from the questionnaire would be for everyone to sit down and discuss their answers at the session. If you have the time and resources, though, you could cull through the answers ahead of time, and type up the responses on a master questionnaire, so that everyone's responses for each question are grouped together. Then, circulate the master questionnaire before the meeting so that people can review the total range of responses.

The latter method requires more time and energy and a more concerted effort. But people will also be discussing issues on a higher plane, and the results may be worth the time investment.

However you get department heads or team leaders to start thinking about indirect competition, the next step is for them to communicate the message to others within the company. This can be done during group sessions using the questionnaire approach or during one-on-one meetings.

When your whole company is organized around a win-win visionary approach to competition and seeks to excel within its own niche, your customers will take notice and the industry will acknowledge you as a leader in your own little corner of world.

*   *   *

HANDS ON

Value Enhancement

Try this little experiment with your flagship product or service. "Explode" it into the following categories:

1. *Pre-sales* — How are customers educated about your product or service?

2. *Sales process* — What does a customer have to do to buy it?

3. *Training* — What kinds of instructional materials do you provide?

4. *Support* — How are customer problems and questions handled after the sale is made?

5. *Repair/Replacement* — How does a customer get a product fixed within and beyond warranty?

6. *Upgrading* — What do customers do when they've outgrown the product or service?

Now imagine yourself as a customer and rate how well your company performs in each category. Devise a standard scale, from one to five, one to ten, or whatever is meaningful. Now ask a range of people in your company, from administrative assistants on up to department heads or team leaders, and try the same experiment. Compare their results, and then ask a few key customers to do the rating test, too. Compare their results with those of your own people.

If certain categories are negative, don't despair. Think of negative results as opportunities for improvement. Repeat this test six months after you've altered your product or service. Chances are, you'll see the kind of significant improvement that results from well-planned value enhancement.

LONG-RANGE VISION

The future is the past in preparation.
— Pierre Dac

Thinking Tough, Walking Tall

I've watched Joe Batten hold an audience of CEOs in the palm of his hand as he explains his brand of "tough mindedness."

When people hear Joe Batten use the phrase "tough minded," they first assume he's a "nuts and bolts" manager dedicated to analyzing and crunching numbers. In fact, nothing could be the further from the truth. The author of the bestselling *Tough-Minded Management*, which has been reprinted in twenty-one languages, and a new book, *Tough-Minded Leadership*, Batten believes that the whole problem with planning today is its focus on numerical analysis and computer models rather than on the "softer," people side of the business. A "tough-minded" leader, according to Joe, is a person who is open, resilient, growing and changing; the kind of person who walks in front of the flock, exemplifying a human-based value system.

"Oh, the numerical analysis has its use," he comments, "but in the hundreds of companies we've worked with, we've seen that leaders who transform their visions into reality truly understand *people* relationships. They have broad, multidisciplinary backgrounds, and understand the sociological and anthropological factors of their companies—concepts foreign to most business people today."

In *Tough-Minded Management,* which was written in 1963 and revised in 1969 and 1978, Batten predicted that in the age of the computer, people would recede into their machines and begin to ignore the human element of maintaining a business. He was also one of the first to warn of the need to balance the human and machine side of running a business.

Twenty years later, John Naisbitt, in his blockbuster book, *Megatrends,* popularized the concept of High Tech/High Touch, noting that the more technical our society becomes, the more we will have the need for humanistic activities—the nurturing of arts and culture, a renewed emphasis on relationships, and a commitment to spiritual pursuits.

"Actually," Joe comments with a chuckle, "the concept isn't new. People whose vision is rooted in reality have understood the human link for some time. Thomas Watson of IBM once surprised the industry by stating that IBM is *not* a technological company. IBM spends most of its time, money and resources on its *human* resources. As a result, its technology is satisfying and profitable.

"Sadly, though," he continues, "lots of companies, especially those of the Silicon Valley, looked at IBM and missed the model. They attempt to become technological giants and ignore the people element. That's why there are so few IBMs today."

Batten insists that an understanding of your own

people extends to an understanding of customers, which in turn serves as the platform for your planning activities. "Real strategic planning means that you help your company see the wisdom of becoming customer-*led* rather than customer-*driven*," he says. "If you're customer-driven, you're in a reactive mode. If the company is customer-led, all information is organized so that the leader can clearly and decisively read his clients or customers. That, too, is part of tough-minded leadership. You're not always right, but you're never in doubt. You must make decisions and go with them!"

Such an approach must shape the planning process, Batten believes: "You won't make anyone money unless you have the tactics to fulfill what client-led information tells you. Without the tactics, planning just amounts to a hollow strategy that says in effect, 'Here, go out and sell this to the customer.' By contrast, if you key every goal and action plan directly to the sensitive data you're getting from the market, you'll succeed. It's just that simple."

*   *   *

Rethinking Long-Range Planning

Every business must carry out some kind of long-range planning if it has any hopes of success. Typically, the planning process involves an annual plan and a three- or five-year plan. In an ideal world, customers would obey the forecast upon which your annual is based, and the marketplace would mold itself to the assumptions of your longer-term plans.

Unfortunately, the world doesn't behave in an ideal way: customers change their minds; equipment breaks down; cutting-edge technologies burst into the market and supplant older ones; the economy takes unexpected twists and turns; political events reshape international markets;

large-scale accidents and natural disasters cause the price of raw materials to soar, etc. In short, change is the only constant in the universe, so the planning process must be flexible for it to be of any value to your company.

Despite the inevitable changes that occur inside a business and the fluctuations that ripple through the world at large, many companies behave as if the universe is static. They cast their plans in stone, and their managers issue edicts to make the plan happen — at all costs. If the sales figures aren't met, heads roll; if a new product doesn't do as well as anticipated, heads roll; if the return on investment doesn't meet expectations, heads roll.

This kind of "number crunching" approach, as Joe Batten calls it, has nothing to do with the real world. It is merely an intellectual game that MBAs play. Real planning has to do with clear-sighted vision and a deep understanding of what makes the marketplace tick. On a macro level, it begins with an inquiry into your assumptions about the marketplace and the immediate environment, and filters down to a micro level, where strategic plans are translated into everyone's daily actions. This chapter focuses on the macro level, while the next chapter of the book brings the planning process down to a personal level.

Synchronizing With Reality

Companies that go purely by the numbers often find that their forecasts and projections are of little value due to the kinds of changes described above. Companies that rely on what Joe Batten calls "customer-led information," on the other hand, are flexible and ready to adapt. By reading the information that pours in through the media, through their sales force and through direct contacts with clients and customers, customer-led companies can immediately respond to the changes that shape the market.

Before such "dynamic planning" can be brought to

bear, though, it is important to establish an information base that describes your initial set of assumptions about your company, your customers, your competitors and your immediate environment. Too often, companies will just look at past performance and assume that the future will be more of the same. Such thinking amounts to fantasy because it disconnects the company from the ebb and flow of the marketplace.

The following three-step planning program will help you develop an information base that you can tap into during the course of the year. You can then modify your short- and long-term plans to match the realities of the marketplace.

Before delving into the program, bear in mind that any useful planning process is also a learning process. While achieving your target goals is certainly important, the real value in the process is learning from your mistakes and learning to do what cognitive psychologist Jerome Bruner calls "going beyond the information given." This means that you start with a set of facts and rules and generalize them to other situations.

In this way, a single collection of facts and rules becomes extremely powerful, enabling you to predict the specifics of many different situations. Thus, you don't have to continually stick your finger in a flame to learn that fire will burn. Similarly, if you enter a market that you know nothing about and get burned, you'll know next time to stick to your knitting.

Step 1: Cutting a Slice of Time

Any time you plan, you're taking a snapshot of the world at a given time. Tomorrow the colors and contours may change. Therefore it's vitally important to record your assumptions about your company and the outside world at the time of your initial planning. As you'll notice in the following list, the subject of inquiry begins at the core of your company — its people — and steadily moves outward to increasingly intangible spheres of influence. Not all of the categories will be relevant to your business — just fill out those items that are appropriate for your company.

For example,

Corporate Sphere

Our People

- Strengths (special skills, dedication, vision, etc.)

- Weaknesses (in terms of knowledge, skills, growth potential, etc.)

- Perceived opportunities for improvement (more one-on-one training, more associates meeting to hone strengths, etc.)

Our Systems

- Strengths (allows people to grow, provides flexibility, provides accountability, etc.)

- Weaknesses (too many bureaucratic layers impede decisions, too much reliance on computers instead of intuition, etc.)

- Perceived opportunities for improvement (streamline management, conduct workshops to boost individual creativity, etc.)

Product/Service Sphere

- Competitive advantages (more features, ease of use, etc.)

- Competitive weaknesses (price, availability, etc.)

- Perceived opportunities for improvement (retool product to be more cost competitive while retaining margins, improve distribution, etc.)

Customer Sphere

- Why they buy from us (best credit terms, best support, etc.)

- What generates their ongoing loyalty to us (confidence that new products will be introduced, continuity of support, etc.)

- What can potentially break that loyalty (decline in product support, lack of modifications to old products or introduction of new lines)

- What we can do to attract new customers (special promotions, "Tupperware"-style education programs, etc.)

- What unmet needs we can fulfill in the future (higher capacity products, products that take advantage of technologies currently under development, etc.)

Market Sphere

- Our current market share

- Our maximum market share

- Length of time to achieve maximum market share

- Monthly expected increase/decrease in market share

Supplier Sphere

- Current relationships (partnership, shared vision, etc.)

- Quality of goods/services supplied (few defects, no inbound inspection required, etc.)

- Areas for improvement (even more efficient communication of orders to minimize lag times, more frequent delivery of goods, etc.)

Our Competitors

- Strengths (excellent commission program for sales force, strong national distribution system, etc.)

- Weaknesses (single product line, difficult credit terms, etc.)

- Likely strategies they will use in near term (price slashing, 2-for-1 deals, etc.)

- Likely strategies they will use in long term (garner more shelf space, direct challenges to our products, etc.)

- Gaps in goods and services they provide (no intermediate models, third-party support, etc.)

Economic Sphere

Domestic Front

- Factors in the domestic economy that affect us today (rise in interest rates, sluggish financial factors, etc.)

- Effect of domestic economic factors that could change in the near term (decline in interest rates, rise in GNP, etc.)

- Effect of domestic economic factors that could change in the long term (increase in unemployment, erosion of market gains, etc.)

International Front

- International economic factors that affect us today (exchange rates)

- Effect of international economic factors that could change in the near term

- Effect of international economic factors that could change in the long term

Social Sphere

- Demographic factors that affect us today (population growth, average marriage age, etc.)

- Effect of demographic factors that could change in the near term (number of women entering the work force, percentage of single men and women, etc.)

- Effect of demographic factors that could change in the long term (baby "boomlet," change in marriage rate, etc.)
- Lifestyle trends that affect us today (average vacations, vacation home-sharing, etc.)
- Anticipated lifestyle changes that could affect us in the near or long term (shift in amount of leisure time, shift in desirable retirement areas, etc.)
- Workstyle trends that affect us (telecommuting, job sharing, etc.)

Legislative Sphere

- Regulations that affect us today (waste disposal, wage laws, etc.)
- Pending regulations that could affect us in the near and long term (tighter emission standards, new OSHA regulations, etc.)
- Proposed regulations that could affect us in the near and long term (changes in tax laws, changes in copyright laws, etc.)
- Other current, pending and proposed legislation that could alter the way we do business

Political Sphere

Domestic

- National political situations likely to affect our business (presidential elections, referenda, etc.)
- State political events that could have an impact on us (increased or decreased appropriations, court appointees, etc.)
- Local political events that might help or hinder the business (local referenda, bans, etc.)

International

- International political events likely to have an impact on our business (new regimes, changes in trade agreements, etc.)

- "Flash points" that could temporarily or permanently alter our ability to do business in certain sectors of the world (civil war zones, coups, etc.)

- Danger zones in terms of kidnapping, assassinations, etc.

The Environmental Sphere

- Natural phenomena that could affect us (storms, floods, hurricanes, earthquakes, etc.)

- Man-made phenomena that could affect us (oil spills, nuclear reactor accidents, etc.)

After you've worked through this list, you'll probably want to add other categories of your own. You should do so. The preceding assumptions are designed to get you thinking about everything that drives your business. By thoroughly evaluating each assumption, you'll develop a good sense of where you're strong and where you're vulnerable, so you can take proper steps to build an even better foundation capable of withstanding the rigors of change that shape the marketplace.

Step 2: Build Your Plans

Sales and Production Plans

Once you've listed your assumptions, you can realistically build your various plans. Your annual sales and production plans will be based on forecasts, which in turn will be founded on historical data. These plans should include contingencies based on what-if scenarios using your list of assumptions.

If, for example, your analysis reveals that a competitor is very likely to experience a general strike in the next six months, run various contingency plans so you have the resources necessary to take advantage of the additional orders that flow your way while the competitor is down. If you plan right, you might even be able to transform some of your new temporary customers into permanent customers. But if you aren't prepared, you may not be able to seize the opportunity, in which case another competitor may benefit from the situation.

Similarly, if you believe that the dollar will steadily increase in value during the next six months, your products may be less attractive to the Europeans, so you'd better prepare for the possibility of reducing your production and distribution plans accordingly. Otherwise, you might get stuck with costly excess-finished-goods inventories or raw materials.

Obviously, it's less expensive to do "what-if" analysis ahead of time with pencil and paper or computer than it is to exploit marketing opportunities on the fly or solve major problems while in crisis mode. Operating in crisis mode always costs more because you pay premium rates for labor and materials. So follow the old adage that says, "The time to make a plan is before you need one."

Strategic Plans

Whereas the sales and production plans are ultimately designed to achieve numerical targets, your long-range strategic plans should take a broader look at the information generated by your listing of assumptions. The strategic plans will call for a certain level of business by a certain date, but more important than hitting a target, the plans should describe the kind of company you would envision yourself running in three or five years.

Perhaps your goal is to be the technology leader in a certain sector of your industry. Perhaps your goal is to be the ultimate customer service company in your field. Perhaps your goal is to become more vertically integrated, so you're less dependent on certain suppliers and able to eventually increase your margins. Whatever the goal, the information you gleaned in Step 1 will be critical toward helping you chart your company's future course.

Here are some questions that have helped my management team formulate and test our business strategy for soundness. I got this line of thought from George Day's book, *Market-Driven Strategy,* then adapted it to fit our needs.

Business strategies are basically set by our choices in these areas. Department heads, enterprise managers and senior management must revisit these basic questions regularly.

1. ARENA

- Which markets to serve?
- Which customer segments to target?
- What is the definition of our business?
- What key success factors (core competencies) must we master?

2. ADVANTAGE

- What differentiates us from competitors?
- How can we increase this differentiation? (Superior value is created when the benefits customers derive from superior performance are worth more than the price they pay. Are we creating superior value? How can we improve?)
- Who is our target competition, if any?
- What new competitive advantages can we develop?
- How will we create satisfied customers? Who will be loyal?

3. ACCESS

- What communication channels to use in reaching the market?
- What method of distribution to use?

4. ACTIVITIES

- What is the scale of the activities to be performed? (How big? How fast to grow?)

- What is the scope of activities to be performed? (Over what geography?)

- What alliances can help us achieve our objectives?

- Are we doing things that, if farmed out to independent contractors, would free up resources we could use to add to our core competencies? (Those things we do best that add value to our products.)

- Should we build, defend or harvest our market position?

Choices in these four strategic areas have a ripple effect on the company. They determine the key success factors. They define the skills needed to mobilize resources. They shape our expectations for profit and growth.

George Day gives us four questions to use in double-checking our chosen strategy:

Test One: Will our strategy create and maintain a competitive advantage through some combination of lowest-delivered cost or superior customer value?

Test Two: Are our assumptions valid?

Test Three: Is the strategy vulnerable to uncertainties? Can these risks be avoided or contained?

Test Four: What are the prospects for successful implementation? (feasibility? supportability? consistency?)

Step 3: Ongoing Review

As mentioned above, one of the great fallacies of planning is that you can do it once a year, then forget about it until next year. The best of plans will quickly become outdated for many of the reasons cited above, the chief one being that customers simply don't comply with your forecasts.

Any successful company will review its plans on a regular basis, depending on its product and the time of year. During peak selling time, you may need to review your plans on a weekly basis to make sure that your production plans are in sync with the marketplace. During a crisis, you might even have to meet daily to develop alternative plans.

At the very least, manufacturing companies should meet once a month to compare the performance of the sales plans with the forecast and to make sure that their production plans are in sync with the market place. Companies that distribute non-manufactured goods should also meet once per month to make sure that their sales and marketing efforts are coordinated with their inventories or suppliers. And companies that offer services only should also meet regularly to take the pulse of the company's strategies for acquiring new customers and maintaining old ones.

Gathering Information for the Review

During the regular review sessions, team leaders or department heads should look not only at internally generated reports (sales, production, profitability, etc.), but they should also examine evidence from a diverse array of information sources and compare it against the assumptions outlined in Step 1. In a small company, each team leader or department head should establish an information flow that ensures a steady stream of vital information each month. The job of gathering and analyzing information can be assigned to individual team members as a regular task.

In a larger organization, or in an organization that operates in a highly volatile environment, it may even be prudent to develop a full-time "information task force" charged with the job of monitoring the marketplace and the primary forces of change that can affect the company.

Information should be culled from a broad range of "cultural media" sources, not just magazines within your own trade, or newspapers from your own area. Put together a balanced "cultural media" digest that ensures people will examine trade and specialty magazines from other industries.

If you're in the building supply industry, see what's happening in the food processing or electronics industries—you never know what you'll find. Perhaps you'll read a clipping that will spark new ideas for seizing opportunities in your own industry, or spotting potential problems that might not even exist yet. Include several regional newspapers or publications from parts of the country in which people are very different from those in your own locale. Again, you might find a key insight that you would have missed by sticking with the known and familiar.

You should also alert people to watch television and listen to radio with their eyes and ears attuned to issues that could affect the business. Consider making up small note pads that people can keep handy in their homes or cars. Each sheet might have a space for the date and time, the source, and the content of the broadcast.

Finally, make sure that your "information task force" or the people who will track basic information keep up with the major business and news periodicals. If they read general publications with an eye to issues relevant to your company's short-term and long-term performance, they'll soon find that they're looking at the world in a new and exciting way.

The information itself can be stored and presented in a variety of formats, depending on the size of your company. You might, for example, wish to create a highly sophisticated computer database that contains data from newspapers, business magazines and trade magazines, and is available on line to people within the company.

At the other extreme, you might want to photocopy key articles and create your own "information gazette" containing information that pertains to the categories you analyzed earlier in Step 1. An in-between approach is to develop a "briefing bulletin" that contains a short abstract of key articles, news broadcasts, etc. The writers or editors of the bulletin should analyze the abstracts and include recommendations for putting the information to use.

However you collect and distribute information, the key is to maintain a steady flow. The phrase "information is power" might be hackneyed these days, but in the business world it still rings true. For as Joe Batten maintains, customer-led companies are really information-based companies; they formulate their strategies on solid information and decisively move forward into the marketplace, ready to test the world against their ideas and assumptions.

Step 4: Make a Decision/Take Action

Once your review has been completed and you have determined that changes in the plans are required, *all* key people should be involved in the decision-making process. In a manufacturing company, for example, if an opportunity to sell more product has suddenly materialized, production people as well as sales and marketing people must decide whether it is feasible to increase the factory output. If product revenues appear to be headed for an unexpected downturn, then sales, marketing, finance and production people should meet to discuss the alternatives.

Even in non-manufacturing settings, every team

leader or department head should be involved in decisions regarding new opportunities or problems that could have an impact on sales or revenues. In today's complex world, autocratic rule is rarely effective; there is simply too much to know, too many factors to be taken into account for one person to manage by himself or herself.

A Decision-Making Model

Assuming that decisions will be made in some kind of democratic fashion, it is critical to understand the dynamics of your company's decision-making process. Decision making, whether it occurs at the boardroom or department level, can be approached through numerous models. One model, which has been successfully used at Oster Communications for the past three years, is based on the framework developed by Andrew S. Grove and described in his excellent book, *High Output Management.*

Grove suggests that everyone involved in the decision-making process be able to answer the following questions:

- What decision needs to be made?

- When does it have to be made?

- Who will decide?

- Who will need to be consulted prior to making the decision?

- Who will ratify or veto the decision?

- Who will need to be informed of the decision?

The process basically involves discussion of all areas of agreement and disagreement about the question at hand. (See the appendix for a decision-making worksheet.) Discussion should involve all members of the organization who hold knowledge regarding the decision, all people who will be affected by the decision, and everyone who will be responsible for securing resources or defending them as a result of the decision. Pre-discussion of the issues provides an opportunity to get facts and opinions on the table at one time.

The second step in the process calls for a clear decision. Once the decision is reached by the group, it needs to be stated in very specific terms, including discussion of its implications for the various areas of the company impacted by the matter.

Finally, the decision needs to be given full support, even by those who disagreed. People are usually more willing to back a decision if they are involved in the process and are given a fair hearing on their inputs and opinions. Grove's model provides feedback to the decision makers, so if the decision appears to have been wrong, free discussion is opened once again and the decision is reviewed. An hour of open discussion about the most logical course of action tends to allow new decisions to be made with a minimum of strife and struggle.

Once decisions are made, they should be backed, given the necessary support, and given a chance before people begin to question and second-guess the basic decision. As George Idiorne remarks in his book, *How Managers Make Things Happen*:

> The very act of making a decision work requires a certain blindness to both the possibility of failure and the closeness of the world to the front door of the executive office. This coolness under fire, this willingness to take risks and accept uncertainty without lapsing into indecisiveness lies behind the success stories of many individuals and firms.

Seizing Opportunities

Once the decision-making process has been established and refined, it can be used to take advantage of opportunities as they present themselves and to alter the company plans so that commitments to required resources can be made.

Every business always has more opportunities than it has resources. Therefore, major opportunities with breakthrough potential should be given your best time and talents. Sometimes this means abandoning immediate, safe, but relatively low pay-back ventures to free up resources with bigger potential. The responsibility to focus the decision-making process on the right issues is vitally important to the growth and development of an organization.

A growing organization needs to explore three types of opportunities:

1. *Additive*: opportunities that require no new resources and simply build on existing people and markets. Examples of additive opportunities would be extending a product line or adding a sales office in a new location.

2. *Complementary*: opportunities that offer something new, perhaps a change in the product line. Complementary opportunities demand new resources, usually new knowledge and areas of competence, either from a technical or marketing perspective.

3. *Breakthrough*: opportunities that change the fundamental characteristics of the business. A breakthrough opportunity requires major investment of resources to put your company in a new marketplace, to revamp an existing product line. A breakthrough opportunity might make a division or product line totally obsolete, so it carries risk. But risk and reward are always indirectly proportional, so the potential reward is sizeable.

One of the critical decisions in an organization is whether or not to pursue the various types of opportunities as they present themselves. Part of that decision will be based on your organization's risk-taking tolerance. To put this in perspective, think about the four types of risks that management expert Peter Drucker describes:

The risk one must accept—the risk that is built into the nature of the business.

The risk one can afford to take.

The risk one cannot afford to take.

The risk one cannot afford not to take.

Sizing up the risk-reward ratio of various opportunities is at the heart and soul of what decision making is all about. Organizations that fail to take risks are inevitably left floundering in the wake of change, doomed to be shaped by external factors and events. Those that take foolhardy risks often find themselves in bankruptcy court or part of another company. The balance lies in taking calculated, carefully qualified risks that are consistent with the company's vision and expertise. Companies that pursue a balanced approach reap ongoing and consistent rewards.

Problem Solving

During your review of the company's plans, you may not always have the luxury of seizing opportunities. Most of the time, in fact, you'll be solving problems. Unlike the decision-making process, which entails probing new territories, the problem-solving process involves dealing with what is known. Also, whereas the decision to pursue opportunities may involve "fuzzy" choices, problem solving also generally involves clear-cut alternatives.

When confronted with a problem, consider using the following framework:

1. *Define the problem in a single sentence.* Problems often take on monumental proportions that seem unsolvable. But the fact is, even the most complex problem can be

boiled down to one sentence without trivializing it. From that one sentence, you can proceed to develop an effective solution.

2. *List everyone who is affected by the problem.* Think of the "problem zone" as a traditional target made up of concentric rings. At ground zero, the bull's eye, list the people and organizations that will be most severely affected. In the next ring, identify the second tier of casualties and continue outward until the entire effect of the problem is clearly mapped out. At that point you will know the extent of the problem.

3. *Rate the type and severity of the problem.* Is it a minor nuisance? Is it likely to go away but come back with even more force at a later date? Is it likely to trigger a string of secondary problems? Or is it a life-threatening situation, the kind in which heads roll and companies become statistics?

4. *Create response scenarios.* Begin with the option of doing nothing. What will happen? If that is not adequate or possible, develop brief scripts or scenarios for various responses, each using escalating commitments of time and resources. Stop with the scenario that seems most effective; solutions that go overboard are often no more desirable than solutions that don't go far enough. The key to developing effective solutions to problems is to think in terms of *appropriate* responses.

5. *Risk action.* Armchair problem solving might be safe, but it never gets you back in the game.

If you follow the three-step program provided in this chapter, you'll maximize your chances of developing a plan that will serve you well in the short and long term. If you communicate the plan and its underlying vision to your associates, they will apply it in their daily work.

It is the day-to-day implementation of the plan that

ultimately results in realizing the organization's bigger vision. Historian Arnold Toynbee once said that the only thing man learns from history is that he doesn't learn from history. In business, you *can* learn from history—if you're attuned to the pulse of the marketplace and take "tough-minded," decisive actions as necessary.

* * *

HANDS ON

Decision Tree

Consider the most important decision made in your company during the past six months. Map the impact of the decision, starting from the point at which it was made to the person most remotely affected. In retrospect, how could the decision have been improved? Draw another decision tree, posing alternatives. Think about ways that the alternative tree could have been used in your company.

Problem-Solving Exercise

Think about a major problem that you've recently encountered in your business or personal life. Analyze it with the problem-solving method described in this chapter. How might you have handled the problem differently? Script several alternatives and think about using them the next time you encounter a similar situation.

THE LEADER'S DYNAMIC VISION

Much that seems incomprehensible today may prove to be the inevitable sequence of all that immediately preceded it.

— Paul Vezelay, British Artist

What's in the Box?

Bob Buford is one of the most practical visionaries I know. He's a member of the Oster Communications, Inc. advisory board, so I have learned to both appreciate and apply his thinking in my own business setting.

"When I was thirty-four years old, I wrote my first set of directions for life," explains Bob, CEO of Buford Television which builds cable systems in eight states. "I was succeeding in business, but in the process of gaining what I was gaining I worried about what I would lose — my intimacy with God, with my wife and with my son."

"I felt that if I drew a set of concentric circles I could put what's most important in the center, and what's less important as I went out. In the center circle, I put my relationship with Christ. In the next concentric circle, I listed things that could be satisfied with relationships. In

185

the third ring, I listed things that can be satisfied by projects and achievements. And in the outermost circle I put those things that can be satisfied with money."

According to Bob, anyone can be consumed by the urgency of tangible needs—you do need money to buy a home, a car and other essentials. But people's priorities change over time, which is why Buford stresses the importance of re-examining key values every year or so, especially when something happens externally.

For Bob, the need to re-evaluate his life became crucial when he lost his son in a tragic accident. "I had planned my life around my son succeeding me in this business," he says. "All of a sudden there was a great emptiness, and I needed to sit back and figure out what my life meant."

Since the accident, Bob has spent much time contemplating the contents of the concentric rings in his life. "Relationships have become even more valuable to me," he comments. "But there are some things that haven't changed: my commitment to serve the Lord, my commitment to remain married to the same person I'm married to now; my commitment to be responsible with my money, not to simply hoard it and spend it on self-indulgent things. These things have remained constant year after year."

Bob applies the same kind of self-evaluation process to his business. "You can grow for your whole lifetime as an individual or company, but you must periodically change the basis of your growth. To maintain your company vision, look at the 'S-life cycle.' Results are on the outside of the 'S' while costs and efforts are on the inside. You have to ask where you are in the life cycle of your current projects. Are you just beginning, or are you topped out? I ask that for every activity I'm involved in."

Once you know where you are on the "S" curve, Buford recommends sponsoring team exercises in which people evaluate all key activities. At his company, teams use a project guidance worksheet that articulates the key priorities of the people involved, the status of the project, and the mission of the project. This tells them whether the vision for the project is on target or has drifted.

The team exercises at Buford's company are complemented by a monthly "Environmental Monitoring Review." "We have a person who compiles a three-page digest of the news that we think will affect us. This includes things like interest rates and the major developments in local economies, regulation, customer preference, etc. The common thread is that these are things that we have no control over, yet they present an opportunity or a threat. We spend a couple of hours after reading the digest and discuss what we think it means to us."

The final phase entails what Bob calls the "President's Forum." "I don't think we're designed individually," he says, "but collectively. So I collect the people I'm involved with and ask them to rate our various systems. If someone says, 'I think we're a seven on marketing,' and someone else says, 'I think we're a two,' that serves as a springboard for discussion. 'Why do you think we're a two on that?' I'll ask. That kind of probing usually leads to fruitful discussion. We frequently revise our staffing after those sessions—add more engineering talent, more marketing people, etc."

Perhaps the most tantalizing of all Buford's techniques for maintaining a clear personal and corporate vision is an exercise he calls "What's in the box?"—what's of ultimate value to you? The impact of this question became apparent about four years ago when Bob hired a well-known strategic planner to help re-evaluate his life and his business. "I talked away and even invited my wife to join me," Bob recalls with a smile. "The strategist then said, 'I've been listening to you for several hours, and for you it's either money or Jesus Christ. Tell me which is in the box and I'll tell you the implications for your strategic planning.'

"So I said after some thinking that of these two, I'd put Jesus Christ in the box. Then he said, 'Sell the company and invest it in the Christian ministries that you've been describing.' I didn't sell the business, but I did see a mid-ground. I could use my business as a platform; everyone needs a platform. In this country, it means 'Who you are is what you do.' I could use my business as a means of generating wealth for causes I believe in.

"I've slowed the growth and now devote more time to a second career, an organization that raises funds for local ministries. By realizing what's in the box, I can now approach the rest of my life like Andrew Carnegie. He decided, while in his early thirties, to make a lot of money and give it all back to society in meaningful ways. I think I'll do the same. For me, that's what the box is all about."

*   *   *

Types of Change

For centuries, thinkers have grappled with the concept of change. The Greek philosopher Heraclitus noted that you can't put your foot in the same river twice. Later on, Aristotle identified two types of change: Transformation occurs when an acorn grows into a tree; momentary change occurs when a leaf falls off the tree. This is a valuable insight for our personal and professional lives because it helps us distinguish between things that have dramatic, long-term effects on our well-being versus things that really have no lasting consequence—"blips" on the computer screen of life.

We can extend that line of thinking into some modern

management advice by another great thinker, Peter Drucker. He said businesses are constantly bombarded by changes from within and changes from without. Pay constant attention to the external factors, Drucker advises, because they're beyond your control.

This chapter focuses on those aspects that you *can* control to some degree, and suggests techniques for maintaining constancy in a sea of change.

A Visionary Grammar

The marketplace, as we saw in the last chapter, never stays still for very long. Customers change, companies change and the world changes — every day, every week and every month. If that's the case, what's the point of developing a vision, which is by definition rooted in time? The answer lies in the words, "rooted in time." A clear-sighted vision is based on values and ideals that can endure, despite changes taking place within and outside the company.

The most enduring of all ideals is the belief that your company will achieve eternal value if it is based on the servant's attitude. As we saw earlier in the book, the servant's attitude is a selfless state in which we exist to help our fellowman achieve his goals. If you begin with that attitude, then it really doesn't matter what happens in the world at large. If the marketplace changes in a way that forces your product or service to change, if competitive pressures, consumer preferences or new technologies require you to shift into a whole new field, the servant's attitude can still give you a distinctive, competitive edge; the ideal is truly "portable" to any field of endeavor.

To return to Bob Buford's metaphor, you must ask, "What's in the center circle?" For those things remain stable regardless of the external situations. You, therefore, become proactive about what's important to you and reactive to the external factors.

At the center of any vision you will find the will to serve. But you must also translate that will into specific actions that people can apply on a daily basis in their work. The translation is achieved through a "visionary grammar" that builds on the core rules of serving.

Consider the value of a grammar underlying a natural language. We don't learn every possible correct sentence when we learn a language; that would be impossible and fruitless. Rather, we learn "generative rules" that allow us to create an infinite number of unique (and correct) sentences. In the same way, a visionary grammar allows us to create an infinite number of unique visions, each of which contains the seeds of the servant's attitude. Here are some rules that will help you develop a clear-sighted vision that endures the course of time.

Think in Terms of Absolute Values

An unequivocal sense of right and wrong will serve as a beacon that guides you through difficult decisions. If your vision grows from absolute values, you will be spared the problems plaguing so many companies today.

People will be able to focus on issues that develop the business rather than debating what constitutes ethical and appropriate behavior. You and your associates will be free from the anxieties that consume so much of our creative energy and swallow our potential. Your path will be easy to follow, because it will be clearly marked with the signposts that have guided man to righteous living for ages.

Practice Fairness

Like trust, fairness is a key ingredient of success. A company that is based on fairness can weather the stormiest of seas. As an example of how a lack of fairness can hurt a company, consider what happened when General Motors's management voted itself a hefty pay raise at the same time that it attempted to secure wage concessions from its unions. The action was considered so unfair and outrageous that GM's management had to reverse its decision and rescind its raises.

In contrast, during a difficult financial period, Levi Strauss's management voted itself a voluntary pay freeze, which bought it the popular support of its labor force. The company survived and grew stronger as a result of its management's eye towards fairness.

Seek the Highest Potential

This rule is a corollary to the preceding one. If your vision is based on process, rather than achieving a certain state, you will never be thrown by change. That's because your business itself will be modeled on change. If you're in a constant state of process, you're also in a maximum state of flexibility. And flexibility is a key factor in flowing with changes in the marketplace.

If people operate from a basis of process, they will feel a "positive state of discontent." In other words, they will feel continually challenged to go beyond the present and create their own futures. Such a "tomorrow orientation" will help your company *anticipate* change, rather than waiting for the future to take its own course.

Shift From Being to Doing

It's not *what* the company is doing, but *how* it's doing it that counts. In this society, unfortunately, we normally turn that around. When we meet someone new, we usually ask, "What's your line?" When someone says that they work for the XYZ Corp, we ask, "Oh, what does XYZ do?" Imagine a world in which people were more oriented toward asking questions such as: "How do you serve your fellowman?" or "How does XYZ Corp embody the servant's attitude?"

Even though most of the world may think in terms of being, you can shift the playing field to doing by refocusing your lens from "end-point" thinking—achieve X by a certain date—to "action" thinking—help customers achieve X state—then find new ways to serve them.

This way of thinking is easy if you bear in mind the point raised earlier: Customers don't buy products or services; they buy solutions. And that applies whether you make microchips or potato chips. As a microchip manufacturer, your goal may be to develop higher power chips at lower costs, helping end users to obtain more computing power on limited budgets. Intel Corp. released such a chip in 1987 called the "SX." This lower cost chip gave more people access to the new "386" generation of computers, which in turn will be required to handle many of the new software programs.

As a potato chip maker, your goal might be to produce and distribute the healthiest product that sates people's appetite for snack food. Perhaps you cut out salt, use less saturated oils or cut out all additives. Cape Cod Potato Chips, a small company based in Hyannis, Massachusetts, began just that way and has gone on to become a regional success.

Develop Trust

Trust is not only a fundamental building block of any business, but it is also an essential ingredient of the creative process. Creativity entails taking risks, and people won't take risks unless they're confident that failure won't lead to reprisals. By fostering creativity, you also ensure the future of your company, for creativity allows you to ride the waves of change.

If the costs of raw materials suddenly rise and threaten your policy of offering top quality goods at a fair price, get creative. Don't just accept cost increases; send an engineer to your supplier's operation and find ways to help *him* cut costs, so he can pass the savings on to you. Black & Decker does just that to keep down the costs of its power tools. That takes trust on the part of both the buying company and supplier because of the risks involved. But the result of such creativity means that all parties involved succeed and prosper.

Stay in a Continual Learn Mode

Companies that roll with the ebb and flow of the marketplace and the world at large are continually learning. They never assume, "We've got it down pat, and it's clear sailing from here on out." They are driven by a vision that says, "Business is a search, and sometimes there's a discovery. And behind every discovery there's yet another discovery to be made."

If you've found the key to a successful marketing strategy, there's probably an even better one to be had. Ask what you can learn from your present success and your past mistakes. If you've improved the efficiency of a manufacturing process, you can probably learn ways to make it even more efficient.

The same holds for *any* aspect of the business. The motivation to learn, though, must be a fundamental aspect of the vision; the vision must instill the curiosity of the child in every person within the company.

Think of the Whole Globe

Every company in the world is part of an organic whole, whether it's a Mom-and-Pop variety store or a multinational conglomerate. Although you may not be making international policy, you do, nevertheless, in some way affect the fate of the world. By setting an example conducting business according to eternal truths, by exemplifying the life of the servant, and by using your God-given talents to their fullest, you are making the ultimate contribution to peace and love on the planet.

*   *   *

HANDS ON

This exercise is modeled on Bob Buford's evaluation process. Draw four circles and indicate in the central circle what's of central importance, radiating outward until you're really dealing with peripheral or temporary issues. When that's done, ask, "What's in the box? What's the central driving force in my business and my life?"

A CHRISTIAN BUSINESS AGENDA FOR THE NEW MILLENNIUM

Since the 1960s we've seen the rise of mysticism from the East and secular humanism in the West. But there's a new movement, too; one that will make its mark in the '90s and beyond. In fact, it's not really new at all; it's the recognition of the basic tenets of Christianity.

It's a recognition that we don't *need* to be mystified to find spiritual enlightenment. It's a recognition that the fear, worry, emptiness and doubt that consumes so much of our creativity can be replaced by the sense of competence, destiny and fellowship which results when a man or woman becomes a follower of Jesus Christ and develops a relationship which is far more powerful than a mere religion.

In our personal lives, the Christian view of the world frees us from fear and emptiness. In our business lives, it makes it possible for work to become a means of building a better society, a better world at large. As we've seen in this book, if you believe that man is a created being of infinite value, you treat your business associates, customers, suppliers and competitors with greater esteem. You assume that they have a special dignity instilled by God, a dignity that can't be taken away.

That high view of man affects an organization in many ways. It impacts a company's values, its personnel policies, its attitude toward right and wrong, its long-range plans, its definition of quality, and its definition of excellence. In short, when you harness the driving energy of a Christian-based vision, you empower the human spirit, enabling people to accomplish great things.

As Christianity is applied—lived out in lives, not just accepted as religion—it will guide us in a new, clear-sighted direction. As more people live as true Christians in their personal lives, they become as transparent channels of spiritual blessings and spread the Christian spirit throughout their businesses.

We will see new levels of satisfaction within the workplace and new levels of achievement in the world at large as this eternal spiritual power is released in society once again. Businesses will become potent forces, joining churches and other volunteer organizations in solving many of society's problems—destitution, homelessness, drugs and many of the other ills that impoverish the lives of so many at home and abroad.

And the signs are very positive. I see a new breed of servants afoot, people who see their company in a new light, as means of creating a better world rather than vehicles solely for personal profit and gain. I see small private companies doing great things to promote fellowship in their immediate surroundings. I see large conglomerates on the scale of IBM allocating more funds to improving society at large.

Across the oceans, in many oppressed nations, there's a fantastic appetite for the truth. Millions of people in politically oppressed nations are turning to Jesus Christ. I see it in the Eastern Bloc. I saw it in the 1980s in China. Recently my wife Carol and I were stunned by the enthusiasm for the gospel in the Soviet Union. The new freedoms include the opportunity to talk about Christ and pass out Christian literature—even inside the very walls of the Kremlin. The church is literally exploding with the truth in these parts of the world. And the new converts who are attracted to Christianity from all parts of the globe exhibit the original fervor of the New Testament church. A spiritual revolution is underway.

I believe that in the next millennium we will begin to feel a fresh impact of Christianity in a global sense. People, infused with the Spirit of Christ, will pour love and energy into their communities, liberating their fellowman from terrible living conditions and other forms of oppression that have accompanied atheistic societies.

You, too, can help the world enjoy the fruit of the Spirit—the love, joy and peace that flow from within when you accept Christ. I believe that the power of Christianity comes when it is treated as a relationship, not as a "religion." Here are four spiritual laws you can follow to establish this relationship and become part of the "new" movement that will shape the new millennium:

1. God loves you and offers a wonderful plan for your life.

   For God so loved the world, that He gave His only begotten Son, that whoever believes in Him should not perish, but have eternal life (John 3:16).

2. Man is sinful and separated from God, therefore he can't know and experience God's love and plan for his life.

   For the wages of sin is death [spiritual separation from God] (Romans 6:23).

3. Jesus Christ is God's provision for man's sin.
Through Him you can know and experience God's
love and plan for your life.

But God demonstrates His own love toward us, in
that while we were yet sinners, Christ died for us
(Romans 5:8).

4. We must individually receive Jesus Christ as
Savior and Lord; then we can know and experience God's love and plan for our lives.

But as many as received Him, to them He gave the
right to become children of God, even to those who
believe in His name (John 1:12).

Open your heart, accept a gift—it's just that simple.

If you would like to know more about Christianity, ask
the publisher about books available on Christianity from
my favorite authors, Dr. Bill Bright, president of Campus
Crusade for Christ, or Josh McDowell, author and speaker.
Their efforts are impacting and changing lives around the
world.

> Here's Life Publishers, Inc.
> P. O. Box 1576
> San Bernardino, CA 92402-1576
> 1-800-950-4457

If you are interested in my speaking schedule or have
ideas on how to improve the presentation of ideas in this
book—jot me a note.

> Merrill J. Oster, President
> Oster Communications, Inc.
> 219 Parkade
> Cedar Falls, IA 50613

Appendix

FORMS FOR ORGANIZING OBJECTIVES AND ACTIONS

Organizational and Personal

Organizational Success Planning

Vision —

- What is the organization's vision? Its unique reason to exist? Its "niche" in the world. Its purpose? What *should be* the organization's vision, reason to exist, niche, purpose?

Strategies —

- What are the organization's strengths and weaknesses? Once the organization's vision is clearly communicated, a vision for each operating entity can be developed to guide its planning. What are its internal and external environments and how are they changing? What are its competitive edges? What are the critical issues and assumptions which, if faced with a proper response, are likely to define the success level of that organization?

Goals —

- Develop a set of "overarching goals" which, if achieved, will implement one or more of the organization's strategies toward the achievement of its overall vision.

Objectives —

- A statement of the key results you want to achieve in a specific time. These key result areas break down the goals into bite-sized pieces and can be identified by enterprise, department and even by specific person in the organization.

Action Plans —

- A step-by-step plan and timetable on how to achieve each of the key results. These plans should be made in view of the organization's vision, strategic strengths, weaknesses and position in the market as well as its overarching goals and objectives.

Priorities —

- A listing, by order of importance, of the jobs to do on the several action plans. Departments, enterprises, divisions and individuals should have a regularly updated set of priorities.

Personal Success Planning

S
T
R
A
T
E
G
I
C

Strategic Thinking—

- What is your purpose? Define your life vision of who you want to be.

Strategies—

- Assessment of your strengths and how to best bring them to bear in this environment.

P
L
A
N
N
I
N
G

Goals—

- What do you want to do in each area of your life to help achieve your life purpose?

Objectives—

- A statement of the key results you want to achieve in a specific time.

O
P
E
R
A
T
I
O
N
S

Action Plans—

- A step-by-step plan and timetable to achieve each of the key results.

Priorities—

- Order of importance of the jobs to do on the several action plans.

To Do—

- That list of activities to complete today.

Action Plan

Objective

Timetable

Method

Control Measure (Quantify, if possible)

Strategic Positioning for

Strengths

Weaknesses

Environment-Internal

Environment-External

Competitive Advantages

Anticipated Changes

Critical Issues

Market Areas to Focus On

Major Approaches to Be Considered

Goals for _____
Year _____

Spiritual	Family
1.	1.
2.	2.
3.	3.
4.	4.
5.	5.
6.	6.
7.	7.

Financial	Mental
1.	1.
2.	2.
3.	3.
4.	4.
5.	5.
6.	6.
7.	7.

Physical	Business/Vocation
1.	1.
2.	2.
3.	3.
4.	4.
5.	5.
6.	6.
7.	7.

Community

1.

2.

3.

4.

5.

6.

7.

Church

1.

2.

3.

4.

5.

6.

7.

Other

1.

2.

3.

4.

5.

6.

7.

Objectives

Time Span _____

Goal to which these objectives relate:

Stated Objective	Timetable	Results Expected
1. _____	_____	_____
_____	_____	_____
_____	_____	_____
2. _____	_____	_____
_____	_____	_____
_____	_____	_____
3. _____	_____	_____
_____	_____	_____
_____	_____	_____
4. _____	_____	_____
_____	_____	_____
_____	_____	_____

Weekly Priority Planner

WEEK OF _____

Date	Activity	Expected Results

Priorities

1.

2.

3.

4.

5.

6.

7.

8.

9.

10.

11.

12.

13.

Time Inventory Analysis

Time Inventory Sheet for Use in Identifying Time Robbers

What I plan to do tomorrow		What I actually did
	8:00	
	8:30	
	9:00	
	9:30	
	10:00	
	10:30	
	11:00	
	11:30	
	12:00	
	12:30	
	1:00	
	1:30	
	2:00	
	2:30	
	3:00	
	3:30	
	4:00	
	4:30	
	5:00	

How much time was used as scheduled? Unscheduled? What were the time robbers that got me off schedule?

_____

_____

To Do

Short Term This week	**Intermediate** The next month	**Long Range** 3-6 months
1.	1.	1.
2.	2.	2.
3.	3.	3.
4.	4.	4.
5.	5.	5.
6.	6.	6.
7.	7.	7.
8.	8.	8.
9.	9.	9.
10.	10.	10.
11.	11.	11.
12.	12.	12.
13.	13.	13.
14.	14.	14.
15.	15.	15.

Decision-Making Worksheet

Clearly State the Issue

Critical Facts

Alternatives – Pros/Cons of Each

Which Alternative Is Best?

What Action Is Required to Implement It?

Problem-Solving Worksheet

State Problem or Condition

Causes

What Will Be Gained/Lost by Solving

Options/Cost of Each

Best Alternative

Action Required to Implement

Professional and Personal Growth

Quantity		Total
_____	**The Best of Ted Engstrom** compiled by Robert C. Larson. A treasury of Dr. Engstrom's best writings on leadership, time management, goal-setting and more. ISBN 0-89840-212-3/hardcover/$16.95	$ _____
_____	**Becoming a Man of Honor** by Merrill J. Oster. A father-to-son gift for those special occasions when you want to share in a permanent form the principles you value. ISBN 0-89840-192-5/$6.95	$ _____
_____	**Becoming a Woman of Honor** by Marilyn Willett Heavilin. A mother-to-daughter gift when you want to share your values in a lasting and memorable way. ISBN 0-89840-193-3/$6.95	$ _____
_____	**Becoming a Woman of Purpose** by Merrill J. Oster. A successful businessman and father offers wise counsel to his daughter on setting goals, solving problems, managing money, developing relationships and more. ISBN 0-89840-245-X/$6.95	$ _____

Your Christian bookseller should have these products in stock. Please check with him before using this "Shop by Mail" form.

Send completed order form to: **HERE'S LIFE PUBLISHERS, INC.**
P. O. Box 1576
San Bernardino, CA 92402-1576

Name _____

Address _____

City _____ State _____ Zip _____

☐ Payment enclosed
(check or money order only)

☐ Visa ☐ Mastercard

_____

Expiration Date _____

Signature _____

For faster service, call toll free: 1-800-950-4457

ORDER TOTAL $ _____

SHIPPING and HANDLING $ _____
($1.50 for one item, $0.50 for each additional. Do not exceed $4.00.)

APPLICABLE SALES TAX (CA 6.75%) $ _____

TOTAL DUE $ _____

Please allow 2 to 4 weeks for delivery.
Prices subject to change without notice.

VDL 284-0